Animals in Schools

New Directions in the Human-Animal Bond
Alan M. Beck, series editor

Animals in Schools

Processes and Strategies in Human-Animal Education

Helena Pedersen

Purdue University Press
West Lafayette, Indiana

ISBN 978-1-55753-523-8
      1-55753-523-2

Library of Congress Cataloging-in-Publication Data
Pedersen, Helena.
  Animals in schools : processes and strategies in human-animal education /
Helena Pedersen.
      p. cm. -- (New directions in the human-animal bond)
  Includes bibliographical references.
  ISBN 978-1-55753-523-8
  1. Human-animal relationships--Study and teaching. 2. Animal welfare--
Moral and ethical aspects--Study and teaching. 3. Humane education. I. Title.
  QL85.P43 2009
  636.0071--dc22
                              2009007094

Cover photo, "turtle on hands" ©Maxlevoyou / istockphoto.com

Contents

Acknowledgments

I am indebted to a number of people who have supported my research behind this book. The most important persons are the students and staff at the schools where I carried out my fieldwork. They made my time in "the field" invaluable not only as a learning experience on which this study relies, but on a personal level as well.

Since this book is a revised version of my Ph.D. dissertation[1] at the University of Gothenburg (the Department of Education), I am extremely grateful to my academic supervisors Bo Andersson and Dennis Beach, who have not only offered unlimited support and inspiration throughout the research process, but also helped me raise the quality of my research approaches, writing, and analyses. Special thanks to Peter McLaren and Elisabet Öhrn whose support I appreciate tremendously. I also thank Torbjörn Tännsjö for extensive and helpful comments on earlier drafts of my research work, as well as Purdue University Press staff and reviewers.

Generous funding from *Jubileumsfonden* at University of Gothenburg gave me the opportunity to spend a semester at University of California at Berkeley, a stay from which my research benefited greatly. I am very grateful to the Graduate School of Education for accepting me, especially John Hurst and Stuart Tannock, and thanks to all participants at the Social and Cultural Studies Proseminar at "Cal." I also thank the Animals and Society Section of the American Sociological Association for honoring me with their Distinguished Graduate Student Scholarship Award 2006.

In Sweden, there are two research networks that have offered helpful viewpoints in the development of this book: The values education network "Värdenätet" and the "Researchers' Network on Education & Sustainable Development." I give special thanks to Ellen Almers and Margareta Svennbeck. Particularly Marianne Dovemark, but also Birgitta Forsman have done a fantastic job reading and commenting on the first draft of my completed dissertation. Karin Gunnarsson commented on a later draft. Thanks also to all other colleagues, friends, and fellow Ph.D. students whose support I have received. Among them I especially want to mention Marianne Andersson, Ingela Andreasson, Julie Andrzejewski, Annika Bergviken Rensfeldt, Alexander de Courcy, Natalie Dian, Helena Eriksson, Peter Erlandson, Lisa Gålmark, Marie Hjalmarsson, Sohail Inayatullah, Katarina Moström, Pia Nykänen, Carrie Packwood Freeman, Colin Park, Lisbetth Söderberg, and Alva Uddenberg. A particular thanks to my friends in Gothenburg who have offered me places to stay overnight during my periodically very frequent commuting.

Finally, I thank Micke for reading my initial drafts of each chapter and helping me get rid of their worst flaws before I circulated the texts to others. And thanks to Rioja, the shelter dog who moved into our home and our hearts during the writing of this book.

Two sections of chapters 5 and 6 ("The capitalist logic of hunting" and "Hunter education") have previously appeared in Pedersen, H. (2008) "We have to kill the animals so that they won't die!" Classroom discussions about hunting as a dimension of ESD, in J. Öhman (Ed.), *Values and Democracy in Education for Sustainable Development—Contributions from Swedish Research*, 145-64 (Malmö: Liber).

Notes

1. Helena Pedersen, *The School and the Animal Other. An ethnography of human-animal relations in education* (Göteborg: Acta Universitatis Gothoburgensis, 2007), Göteborg Studies in Educational Sciences 254.

Critical animal studies and education research: A background

The intention with the present book is to describe what is actually taking place in classroom settings whenever human-animal relations are brought into focus. It is an attempt to capture and critically analyze a variety of practices through which human-animal relations are configured, mediated, and negotiated within the school context. The schools investigated offer vocational programs in animal care, as well as theoretical programs in the humanities, social sciences, and natural sciences at the upper secondary level. The primary purpose of the study is to explore how schools deal with animal-related issues by studying what messages and "stories" about animals and human-animal relations are expressed (explicitly or implicitly) in the school environment. The focus is on social processes involved in students' and teachers' meaning-making of animals as abstract categories or as embodied beings. I also place these phenomena in a wider social context by exploring how daily classroom activities and interactions may be understood within a larger human-animal related ideological framework, and how human-animal relations may intersect discursively with relations toward *human* "others." By investigating these issues from cross-curricular perspectives and from a critical ethnographic approach,[1] the study aims at making a contribution to the field of human-animal studies as well as to education research.

The book begins with a theoretical background that locates the study

1

of human-animal relations within a framework of critical education research. Then follows part I, comprising three chapters that discuss how animals may figure in identity-shaping processes taking place in school. Chapter 1 deals with identities and conceptualizations ascribed to animals, chapter 2 focuses on how students' professional identities as animal caretakers are influenced by their socialization into certain human-animal relations in school, and chapter 3 discusses the professional role of the teacher involved in human-animal education.[2] These three chapters lay a foundation for the understanding of the various messages and "stories" about animals that take shape in school. In part II, a range of situations in which students encounter animals and human-animal relations are described and discussed. Chapter 4 deals with the visual encounter of animals in zoos, on film, and during field excursions. Chapter 5 focuses on how animals and human-animal relations are commodified and transformed into economic objects in human society, and how school is part of these processes. Chapter 6 explores how the school handles the issue of killing animals for various human purposes. The book concludes with part III, where some primary processes and strategies of human-animal education, as they have emerged in this book, are identified and critically analyzed.

Studying the ways in which we make sense of and use animals is a way toward understanding fundamental features of our society. Philo and Wilbert (2000) note that humans' lives are intertwined with relations to animals to such an extent that animals are even constitutive of human societies in multiple ways. From material as well as symbolical perspectives, animals are a central part of what humans are and what we do in the world and, at the same time, animals and their life conditions are dramatically affected by human actions. At a structural level, animals also enter literally into our politico-economic stories of progress and development (for instance, in the circulation of animal bodies and body parts in globalized commodity chains, or in the genetic trans-figuration of animals in biotechnology), but in the process the animal itself is often rendered physically as well as morally invisible (Emel & Wolch 1998). I am thus primarily concerned with the critical dimensions of human-animal studies. Critical animal studies is a field of research dealing with issues re-lated to the exploitation and liberation of animals; the inclusion of animals in a broader emancipatory struggle; speciesism; and the principles and practices of animal advocacy, animal protection, and animal-related policies (Brock University 2007; ICAS 2008). My approach to critical animal studies involves analytic exploration of social structures, institutions, practices, and ideologies that define what relations are possible between humans and animals and that reduce human-animal interaction to modes and processes of production and consumption. I also seek to scrutinize and problematize a variety of power arrangements by which both humans and animals are currently subjected to domination, marginalization, and exploitation. For this purpose, I rely on a critical theoretical and critical pedagogical framework.

Critical researchers are guided by questions about whose interests are served by particular institutional arrangements and forms of knowledge production, and where our frames of reference come from (Kincheloe & McLaren 1998; Åsberg 2001). By examining the interplay between structure and social practices, critical theory attempts to explain the ways in which dominant ideologies permeate everyday interpretative frameworks (Held 1980). Applying critical theory to the education context, critical pedagogy sees society as fundamentally divided by unequal power relations (Burbules & Berk 1999; Kanpol 1999) and views schooling as a preparation and legitimation of particular forms of social life (McLaren 1998; Kanpol 1999). One aim of critical pedagogy is to challenge value structures that lead to oppressive, alienating, and subordinative social practices, and raise questions about how these are reproduced in school (Kanpol 1999). In Giroux's (1997a) words, this means to highlight how schools function in the shaping of particular identities, values, and histories by producing and legitimating specific narratives. Development of a critical consciousness is thus central in critical pedagogy as is the creation of possibilities for transformative action. Examples of education scholars who have combined critical pedagogy with a critical animal studies approach are Selby, 1995; Andrzejewski, 2003; Kahn, 2003; McLaren & Houston, 2005; and Andrzejewski, Pedersen & Wicklund, 2009.

The critical animal studies perspective is reflected already in the works of the Frankfurt School, where an explicit critique of animal exploitation is found (see Horkheimer 1947; Adorno 1974; Marcuse 1991; Adorno 2000; Horkheimer & Adorno 2002). The following example from the *Dialectic of Enlightenment* illustrates this point:

> Unreasoning creatures have encountered reason throughout the ages—in war and peace, in arena and slaughterhouse, from the lingering death-throes of the mammoth overpowered by a primitive tribe in the first planned assault down to the unrelenting exploitation of the animal kin[g] dom in our own days. This visible process conceals the invisible from the executioners—existence denied the light of reason, animal existence itself. (Horkheimer & Adorno 2002, 245-46)

Not only the exploitation of animals as such, but also the interconnections between the subordination of human and animal "others" are recognized in Adorno's *Minima Moralia. Reflections from damaged life* (1974):

> Indignation over cruelty diminishes in proportion as the victims are less
> like normal readers, the more they are swarthy, 'dirty', dago-like. This
> throws as much light on the crimes as on the spectators. Perhaps the
> social schematization of perception in anti-Semites is such that they do
> not see Jews as human beings at all. The constantly encountered assertion
> that savages, blacks, Japanese are like animals, monkeys for example,
> is the key to the pogrom. The possibility of pogroms is decided in the
> moment when the gaze of a fatally-wounded animal falls on a human
> being. The defiance with which he repels this gaze—'after all, it's only
> an animal' – reappears irresistibly in cruelties done to human beings, the
> perpetrators having again and again to reassure themselves that it is 'only
> an animal', because they could never fully believe this even of animals.
> (Adorno 1974, 105)

Other critical animal studies scholars have broadened our understanding of
human-animal relations by applying central Marxist ideas. Speaking about
human-animal relations of production, Tapper (1988) extends the concept of social relations of production across the species barrier and argues that any set of
ideas about the relation of humanity to animals is a function of fundamental
economic imperatives (conditioned by the socio-political environment). The
production systems Tapper analyzes are hunting and gathering, pastoralism,
agriculture, and urban-industrial production.

Noske (1997) develops a detailed Marxist analysis around the latter
form, building primarily on the concept of alienation. Also Perlo (2002) suggests that not only the concept of alienation, but even the capacity for sympathy in Marxism as well as the theoretical ideas of surplus value and historical
materialism are all applicable to human-animal relations. Similarly, Dickens
(2003) discusses the importance of analyzing human-animal relations within
a historical materialist framework:

> Commodification, capitalism's restless search for value and the
> incorporation of nature of all kinds into capitalist labor-processes, is the
> heart of the capitalist enterprise. Animals as well as human beings seen
> from this perspective are not only, or simply, a "working class" on whose
> labor the whole of human society is predicated. Their biologically inherited
> powers of growth and reproduction are now increasingly subsumed
> within, and indeed modified by, capitalist social relations. They are being
> increasingly modified in capitalism's own image. /.../ Nonhuman animals,
> therefore, no longer are just slaves or beasts of burden, but they increasingly
> are being made central as means of production, ways in which surplus
> value is being realized by applying human labor (in, say, the laboratory)
> to the animals' powers of reproduction and development. /.../ These
> developments are just part of an attempt to make new labor-processes
> out of reproduction. They are no less than new ways of interacting with

> nature to generate surplus value, again using human and non-human labor
> as a free input to realize value and profits. (Dickens 2003, 1)

Marxist perspectives in contemporary human-animal studies and the writings of the Frankfurt School have provided a conceptual basis for my critical ethnographic investigation.[3] Two other important influences that have inspired the present study are gender and postcolonial theory. What follows is a very brief outline of some human-animal perspectives in feminist and postcolonial thought.

Feminist researchers differ with regard to their willingness to exclude or include animals in their discourse. Noske (1997) and Smith-Harris (2003) report about their personal experiences of their involvement in human-animal studies as feminist scholars:

> While researching this book [*Beyond Boundaries: Humans and Animals*] I was once asked at a party in Amsterdam what exactly I was doing. I mentioned my interest in the human-animal 'interface'. The reaction was one of sheer horror. Such research was bound to work against women! As it turned out the continuity question especially was a taboo subject among feminists. Behind my back doubts were expressed as to my political correctness… (Noske 1997, 171)

> When I first became interested in Human-Animal Studies (HAS) many feminist friends warned me not to get involved in research in this area. They discussed the political repercussions of being marginalized from the debates that "really mattered"- those addressing the oppressions connected to humans. (Smith-Harris 2003, 85)

The agenda within feminism that shaped Noske's and Smith-Harris's experiences has been heavily criticized from within the field of feminist studies itself. For instance, Gruen (1993) argues that a failure to address oppressive practices toward animals is to contribute to a reproduction of an exclusionary theorizing that conflicts with basic feminist ideas. Moreover, the categories "woman" and "animal" serve the same symbolic function as "other" in patriarchal society (Gruen 1993; cf. Adams 2002). These connections have been analyzed, for instance, within a gender perspective of meat production and consumption, within the context of domestic (and other) violence toward women and animals, and in ordinary language use in patriarchal society, which tends to produce and reinforce the subordinate status of women and animals (e.g., Dunayer 1999; Adams 2002).

Ecofeminist theory has developed similar critique. Although there are divergent viewpoints, for instance, on the status of animals also within ecofeminism, ecofeminist theory builds on the idea that there are connections between the exploitation of animals/nature and other oppressive practices organized around categories such as gender, race, and class. According to Warren (2000), oppressive practices and structures rely on narratives that explain, sustain, and legitimate relations of domination and subordination in society and include value hierarchical and value dualistic thinking (expressed in categories such as soul/body, reason/emotion, culture/nature, man/woman, human/animal). The links between anthropocentric and androcentric worldviews are thus made explicit in ecofeminist thought.

Intersections of feminist/queer theorizing and human-animal relationships have been further explored by Birke, Bryld and Lykke (2004) and McKay (2005) by building on Judith Butler's analyses. Birke, Bryld and Lykke (2004) use Butler's notion of *performativity*. They see non-human otherness as a *doing* or *becoming* that is produced and reproduced by discursive practices and processes in specific contexts of human-animal interaction and consolidated by repeated action over time. Like gender performativity, species (my term) performativity *creates* a human/animal divide and reproduces relations of power through different inferiority-producing strategies. McKay (2005) applies another notion by Butler, "compulsory heterosexuality" and the constitutive nature of exclusion, to human-animal relations and the discourse of speciesism.[4] Just as binary gendering of the human being locates the gay or lesbian body as the constitutive outside of "compulsory heterosexuality," the animal body may, by means of analogous logics of heterosexism and speciesism, be viewed as the constitutive outside of what McKay terms "compulsory humanity": "It is compulsory that we 'become' human, and this /.../ is a function of our renunciation of the animal" (218).

Like feminist theorizing, postcolonial studies have been criticized for their lack of interest in the "animal connection." One reason for the absence of this interest may be a concern about presumed dangers of destabilizing the human-animal divide and a concern that a focus on animals may trivialize the suffering of human beings under colonialism (Armstrong 2002). Armstrong argues, however, that there are common grounds in postcolonial and human-animal studies. In his view, the idea of the human being's absolute difference from, and superiority over, the animal is connected to colonial legacies. Furthermore, the definition of "the animal" is inextricably bound up with the formation of other notions that are fundamental to the colonialist project, such as "the human," "the natural," and "the cultural" (Armstrong 2002). Referring to Fiddes (1991), Armstrong (2002) gives the example that the "civilizing" mission of European colonialism involved a domination of both "savage" cultures and "savage" nature. In this manner, the "civilized" has been constructed in contrast with the savage and the animalistic in Western history. Accordingly, speciesism is used to underpin racism and slavery, for instance, when "the animal" is deployed as a derogatory term in genocidal and marginalizing discourses (Tiffin 2001). Subsequent chapters will give examples of the appearance of animals in racialized discourse, and how the racialized human subject figures in the discourse of species in connection with human and animal identity production in, for instance, zoos, wildlife films, and animal agribusiness. It will be shown that the colonialist project's striving to justify itself as *benign* and to mask its own oppressive character (Lundahl 2005) is operative also in human-animal relations, and that this strategy finds certain expressions in the school context.

There are weak points in colonialist rationales. Postcolonial discourse in Homi Bhabha's theorizing indicates an uncertainty in the "master identity" of the colonizers, revealed in the way colonialism seeks to produce colonial subjects who are at once "the same" as their colonizers (amenable to cultural assimilation) and "different" from them (amenable to colonization). This implies that the stereotype of "the other" that colonialism relies on is, in fact, unstable and needs to be constantly reinforced in order to remain powerful (Macey, 2000). Oscillations between "similarity" and "difference" are also manifested in various configurations of human-animal relations (Desmond 1999; Bousé 2000), which could imply that also the narratives supporting human domination over animals are inherently unstable and need to be continuously repeated and recreated to maintain authority.[5] (For an in-depth analysis of the animal question in relation to Bhabha's theorizing, see Wolfe [2003b].)

Another perspective is provided by what Armstrong (2002) calls "colonialism's offspring," that is, globalization, and, I would add, cultural, economic, and technological imperialism. This form of reinvented colonialism has not, in Haraway's (2004c) view, appropriated and assimilated organisms as much as it has *remade* them in the image of commodity production.

One element emerging from the critical theories outlined above is what has been called "standpoint theories" in feminist research. Standpoint theories, influenced by Marxist thought, claim to represent the world from a particular socially situated perspective and to represent the social world in relation to the interests of oppressed groups (Anderson 2004). Drawing on feminist epistemology, the ecopedagogue Richard Kahn has argued for an "animal standpoint theory." The quotations that follow are my reconstruction of Kahn's elaboration of this notion as it emerged in an e-mail-based discussion in 2004:

> Standpoint theory is a methodology that is designed to handle the issue
> of power and hegemony /.../ [It is] an attempt to articulate the standpoint
> of the oppressed and marginalized, the counter-hegemonic, hoping
> thereby to increase the objectivity of research discourse by bringing
> into the arena views that have been historically repressed. /.../ [V]ia an
> animal standpoint, one could enlarge the research domain by providing
> perspectives that transgress the dominant order, critique it and reconstruct
> it. /.../ Animal standpoints honor (my term) subjectivity of animals. This
> means that 1) they articulate that animals are sentient subjects of a life, 2)
> they do this because the dominant research and social paradigm denies
> and suppresses this, and so 3) articulating animal subjectivity is part of a
> political project that seeks to transform historical oppressions that cause
> animals to be treated/perceived as objects and not subjects. /.../ The point
> is (…) to articulate the question of oppressor/oppressed relations (and
> the researcher's involvement in them) as part of the research question/
> domain. (Kahn 2004)

Standpoint theories in general have been criticized, for instance, for their tendency to universalize (Birke 1994). Particularly an animal standpoint theory
raises questions about the extent to which it is possible to imagine the experience of "the other," not least from my own position as a researcher belonging
to a privileged species, race, and class. Nonetheless, I see Kahn's outline above
as helpful for articulating a critical dimension in human-animal studies and
these ideas have provided inspiration throughout my project.[6]

This book thus seeks to challenge "conventional," utility-oriented wisdom about human-animal relations and the position of animals in society,
and provide perspectives that reach beyond such paradigms. These perspectives should be viewed in relation to an understanding of the school as not
only an agent of socialization and social and cultural reproduction, but also
as a site where conflicting political values and practices are enacted and contested (Giroux 1997b). In critical education theory, the concept of "the hidden
curriculum" is central to this discussion. I refer to the hidden curriculum as
intended or unintended teaching or learning effects of schooling that are not
stated as aims in formal documents, but form parts of a socialization process
into certain human-animal relations. I have attempted to follow the operating
processes of hidden curricula in different educational settings and acknowledge the interrelations of microstructures, macrostructures, and practices in
and outside the school environment in the formation of these processes (cf.
Martin 2001).

My critical ambition is rooted in Marxist epistemology that focuses on
the material and economic basis of different forms of subordination and exploitation in society (cf. Nibert 2002), but also in Foucauldian ideas of how

subject positions are constituted and negotiated in relation to normalization processes (cf. Carabine 2001).[7] These points of departure relate to different conceptions of power that will be further discussed in the subsequent sections. I will begin with brief accounts of two other key concepts: The animal as "other" and as "social representation."

The animal as "other"

Addressing human-animal relations, Philo and Wilbert (2000) speak about conceptual and geographical forms of "othering," where "conceptual othering" denotes setting animals apart from ourselves in terms of character traits, and "geographical othering" means the physical fixing of animals in places and spaces different from those occupied by humans. In human-animal studies, the animal often figures in accounts of how dichotomies of humanity/animality are constructed in mutual interdependence. This understanding of the other surfaces in, for instance, analyses of how oppressive practices toward human and animal others may intersect and reinforce each other by reliance on similar logics. Wolfe (2003c) remarks that the discourse of speciesism can be used to mark *any* social other. In this context, animals may be viewed as *archetypical* others not only because of their perceived radical difference from ourselves, but also because certain arrangements of oppression toward animals have been used as a model and inspiration for the oppression of human beings (e.g., Patterson 2002). Wolfe (2003c) argues that as the object of both discursive and institutional speciesist practices, the view of the animal as "other" has particular power and durability in relation to other discourses of otherness.

There are some general problems with the notion of the "other." It may balance on the verge of essentialism, evoking an idea of a core of inherent, stable characteristics of individuals. Its frequent use also risks consolidating the binary oppositions of "self" and "other," stigmatizing certain individuals or groups of individuals as stereotyped "others" rather than rendering such discursive markings problematic or dissolving them.

Furthermore, there are divergent views on whether an animal may at all be ascribed the status of "other." In the phenomenological philosophy of Emmanuel Levinas and the symbolic interactionist perspective of George Herbert Mead, an animal cannot be an "other" since animals are presumed to lack fundamental characteristics in their relations to humans. Levinas's and Mead's ideas have been revisited and challenged from aspects of human-animal interaction by contemporary philosophers and sociologists (e.g., Alger & Alger 1997; Clark 1997; Myers 2003; Wolfe 2003a), but the notion of animal otherness has also been questioned from less anthropocentric perspectives than Levinas's and Mead's. Steeves (1999) senses a shared physical existence between beings that leads him to negate space as an element separating individuals, thereby also negating otherness as such from a phenomenological perspective:

> Space tricks us; false philosophy tricks us. My hand reaching for yours seems to move away from me, though it never does: it is me. Your hand, your paw, seems to be There and, hence, other. It is not: it, too, is me. We have met the animal's body, and he is us. There are no animal Others. (Steeves 1999, 8)

Within the critical theory framework applied in this book, however, animal and human otherness is viewed as a useful analytical concept for investigating identity production, normativity, and power arrangements in society (particularly in formal education). My approach also follows feminist theory in the recognition that different animals may be *created* as others in different ways and contexts, and that these processes need to be more closely examined (Birke 1995; Birke & Parisi 1999; Birke, Bryld & Lykke 2004). This makes the issue of animal otherness not only a theoretical tool, but also part of the very objectives of the present investigation.

Social representations, constructions and positions

According to Chaib and Orfali (1995), social representations are collectively developed ideas and conceptions about various phenomena that surround us. They possess a long-term stability that distinguishes them from, for instance, attitudes. Social representations are historically and culturally contingent and derive from dimensions of contemporary society such as politics, science, and mass media, and their function is to produce "commonsensical" knowledge that guides collective forms of social behavior. Social representations may be seen as a "system of values" in the sense that they contribute to the establishment of a social order, and also facilitate communication by providing linguistic codes for describing and classifying social phenomena (Chaib & Orfali 1995).

    When applied to human-animal relations, our way of making meaning of animals is deeply contingent upon the symbolic roles or representations we ascribe to them. Despite their relative stability, social representations and constructions[8] may shift over time and place and can be powerful in that they shape our commonsensical, taken-for-granted understandings of animals: In Arluke's and Sanders's (1996) words, "they do nothing less than shape our consciousness" (16). Through these processes, representations of animals may shape and give meaning to our personal and collective lives and identities (Emel, Wilbert & Wolch 2002; Alger & Alger 2003). The view of non-human primates in the West, for instance, has shifted in the twentieth century from being alien or strange creatures to almost humanlike with complex cognitive and social abilities (Arluke & Sanders 1996). Another shift in social representations is exemplified by the rat, metaphorically transformed from being a disease-bearing, filthy animal of the sewers to a symbol of modern (Western) medical and scientific progress in the *conquest* of disease (Birke 2003) (although both representations may exist simultaneously).

Animals as social constructions and representations can be analyzed on the species level as well as on the individual level. On the species level, Elstein's (2003) analysis of the species concept suggests that it has a subjective and contextual character. He argues that the category of species is not a static, "given" concept but is interest-relative, that is, it has been constructed on the basis of its usefulness in certain contexts rather than on evidence that it possesses certain universal or essential "core" characteristics. According to Elstein, interpretations of species distinctions may actually differ between cultures as well as between scientific communities.

On the level of the individual animal, Marvin (2005) sees all viewing of animals as shaped by social and cultural factors, and argues that "[t]here is no asocial or acultural platform on which we can stand to see an animal as that animal really is" (6). According to Marvin, an animal is represented the moment it is recognized as an animal and can never be simply a neutral presence. Similarly, Baker (2001) writes that there is no unmediated access to the "real" animal (which is not to be taken as a denial of the animal's experience or circumstances, but rather as emphasizing that animals can only be related to through our representations of them).

In this book I focus on social processes that shape constructions and representations of animals. My intention is not to use social representations for making ontological truth claims about animals, but as critical analytic tools for interpreting the processes by which certain (animal and human) categories and individuals become "legitimately" subjected to abusive or oppressive practices. Here, I find Nibert's (2003) notion of "social positions" particularly useful. In his analysis, ascribing social positions to others (humans or animals) may be seen as a way of collective and personal devaluation, which is one element in processes of exerting systematic oppression. Depending on the particular functions various animals fulfill in human society, they are ascribed different social positions in order to consolidate and reproduce these functions. In Nibert's example from early agrarian society, common social positions were "slave" and "serf" for humans and "livestock" and "game" for animals. "Zoo animal" and "lab animal" are other examples of social positions ascribed to animals that are still widely accepted. Nibert's (2003) account of social positions indicates how human society has subjected animals' entire existence to the principles of utility and social division of labor. It is thus above all the morally charged and action oriented dimension of social representations that promotes and justifies certain treatment of animals (Arluke & Sanders 1996). How these dimensions are articulated and processed in the school environment is of particular significance to this book.

Human-animal power relations

The concept of "power" is multifaceted. Numerous definitions of power (most of which center around the human subject) are in circulation in contemporary social research, among which Foucauldian interpretations have probably been the most influential. My primary concern here is to discuss how animals figure in power structures and processes and what understandings of power are implicated. I will focus in particular on how Foucauldian perspectives of power may illuminate our understandings of human-animal relations.

One dimension of power highlighted in critical theory is *domination*. To Horkheimer and Adorno, human beings have a fundamental intention to dominate and master nature that underlies the way both social and natural worlds are appropriated and apprehended (Held 1980). Held remarks that Horkheimer and Adorno did not define the concept of domination but suggested a "minimal condition" for its application, that is, "a situation in which the thoughts, wants and purposes of those affected by (domination) would have been radically different, if it had not been for the effects (it) created." (Held 1980, 148-49)

While the concept of domination seems to extend to animals in critical theory, the notion of *hegemony* is different since it does not operate by force but rather through ideology and the "superficial" consent of the population (Femia 1987). Stibbe (2001) notes, however, that hegemony affects animals in an indirect manner since "the coercive power used to oppress animals depends completely on a consenting majority of the human population who, every time it buys animal products, explicitly or implicitly agrees to the way animals are treated" (147).

Power may be viewed as stemming from different societal groups, such as one group having the ability to exert its will over another (cf. Nibert 2002), or, in a more Foucauldian sense, as being entangled within social organization itself. The former view is embraced by ecofeminist thought, which often conceptualizes power as patriarchally based "power over" human and non-human others. Birkeland (1993) argues, for instance, that we must "move beyond" power and challenge the very idea of power structures as a necessary concomitant of human society.

From a Foucauldian perspective, the exercise of power is not simply a top-down relationship between individual or collective actors, and a society without power relations can only be an abstraction (Foucault 1983). Power is, in this sense, deeply connected to the concept of discourse and may be formulated as "a network of boundaries that delimit, for all, the field of what is socially possible" (Hayward 2000, 3). Power, however, is not only delimiting, it can also be productive. In this sense, power may be viewed as a process that infiltrates both the fine textures of social existence and self-identity (Olssen 2004), also in our relations to animals. Although Foucault never directly addressed human-animal power relations (Palmer 2001), there are examples of works that analyze certain situations of animals in human society and wildlife management in terms of Foucauldian notions such as government (Patton 2003), bio-power and discipline (Williams 2004; Bergman 2005; Novek 2005; Shukin 2009). Palmer (2001) develops a general framework for applying Foucauldian thought to human-animal relations:

> A Foucauldian approach would accept that while there might be what we can think of as globalized human/animal oppressive structures, these have come about by the colonizing of existing heterogeneous discourses and micro-practices, and it is these discourses and practices on which we should focus. So we might approach such an analytic of power by considering the diverse nature of human/animal power relationships and how differently situated they can be /.../ Looked at from this perspective, there are a huge variety of power relationships between humans and animals, with their own instabilities and points of resistance. (Palmer 2001, 350-51)

Palmer distinguishes between *constitutive*, *internalized*, and *external* practices of human power over animals. *Constitutive* practices such as domestication, selective breeding, and biotechnology affect the biological constitution and form of animals, inscribing preferred physical and behavioral characteristics on the genetic make-up of the animal body. *Internalized* practices are human disciplinary practices that affect the subjectivity of animals, such as techniques of training and taming. *External* practices affect the external bodies and/or circumstances of animals. Some examples are confinement, castration, physical punishment, eviction from habitat, and a wide variety of uses of space as a fundamental element in the exercise of power (Palmer 2001; cf. Philo & Wilbert 2000).

The effects of human-animal power relations are symbolic as well as material, and often contradictory. Taking the example of animal agriculture, Burt (2006) discusses the widespread distribution of modernist technologies that have not only been put to efficient use in the regulation, control, and taking of animals' lives within regimes of food production, but also frequently mask these new forms of control as humane and progressive improvements (e.g., modern slaughter techniques). At the same time, responsibility within the food production system is diffused so that no single individual can be held wholly responsible for the harm caused to the animals (cf. Vialles 1994). In this manner, notions of "humane" slaughter, clinical hygienic procedures, scientific efficiency, standardization, and economic optimization come neatly together under a regime of control that makes entire systems of the mass killing of animals for human consumption possible (Burt 2006).

Following Nibert (2002, 2003), this book largely locates human-animal power relations within the dynamic of capital accumulation, or what Palmer (2001) refers to as "globalized human/animal oppressive structures," where animals as a group are systematically oppressed and exploited for economic purposes. Particularly in the micro-practices (in this book, the micro-practices of the school) within which these structures are articulated, enacted, negotiated, or contested (cf. Palmer 2001), I am inspired by Foucauldian perspectives to understand how subject positions are produced to create both hegemonic consent to *and* resistance toward dominant discourses of animals in human society. Following Willis and Trondman (2000), the ethnographic chapters that follow attempt to address the notion of power as being lodged within taken-for-granted meanings and everyday practices as they are lived, experienced, and handled by various actors in school.

Notes

1. The empirical research behind the book builds on a field study carried out in four Swedish upper secondary schools (students sixteen to eighteen years old). The first phase of the study involved twelve semi-structured interviews with students, teachers, and school leaders that took place between September and November, 2003. The second phase involved an ethnographic study including eighty-eight days of participant observation studies, analyses of policy documents, learning materials and other artefacts in my field schools, and informal interviews and discussions with students and teachers that took place between March and December, 2004. Two of the schools offered vocational programs in animal care (with approximately two hundred students at each school with female students being in the majority), designed to prepare students for professions in areas such as zoos, pet shops, wildlife

management, veterinary clinics, and so on. These schools kept animals at the school premises for educational purposes. The other two schools (with approximately one thousand students each) did not have this animal care specialization. These schools focused on university preparatory programs in the humanities/social sciences and the natural science/technical sphere, respectively. All personal names used in the empirical material in this book are fabricated.

2. I use the term human-animal education to denote any situation in school when human-animal relations are brought up or discussed.

3. For a more detailed account of critical theories in relation to animals and biopolitics, see Shukin (2009).

4. There are several definitions of the term speciesism. In McKay's (2005) interpretation, it can denote both an ideology and a discourse that polices the human-nonhuman boundary. The understanding of speciesism as an ideology is proposed by Nibert (2002). According to him, speciesism (like racism, sexism, and classism) is a set of widely held, socially shared beliefs that results from and supports oppressive social arrangements. Wolfe (2003c, 2003d), on the other hand, defines speciesism primarily as an institution, that is, a network of specific modes and practices of materialization that reproduce the objectification of the other on the grounds of species affiliation. In his view, the discourse of species relies on and reproduces the institution of speciesism (Wolfe 2003c). My use of the term speciesism includes dimensions of both ideology and discourse as well as of social arrangements, institutions, practices, and relations.

5. For instance, by giving the example of the zoo, Anderson (1998) argues that the variety of ambiguous responses commonly evoked in zoo visitors upon encountering captive animals (including excitement, sadness, wonder, unease, guilt, nostalgia) reflects a fragility in human-animal power relations. (See also Tiffin 2001, on "hidden or repressed guilt" [39] as a common feature of colonial and human-animal relations).

6. My understanding of Kahn's view is that recognition of animal subjectivity is a central position in animal standpoint theory, but I do not take this to imply that oppressive practices toward animals rely solely on a denial of their sentience. As Williams (2004) has argued, animal sentience can actually be taken advantage of, for instance, by animal industries in order to intensify production.

7. The link between Marxist and Foucauldian social theory lies, according to Olssen (2004), above all in a critical view of domination that takes social practices as transitory and intellectual formations as associated with power.

8. Social representations and social constructions can be distinguished by defining representations as developing from the social constructions that society builds on (Chaib and Orfali 1995), but in this book I will use both terms as largely synonymous.

PART I

The emergence of educational "animal stories"

Human-animal relations were taught in a variety of forms and contexts in the schools I visited—despite the fact that these issues are absent from the national curriculum, Lpf 94 (the National Agency for Education, 2006) that guides formal education in Sweden. In the vocational animal caretaker programs, where I spent most of my fieldwork time, human-animal relations more or less permeated most natural science or animal-related courses, although the values dimension was not always made explicit, but conveyed as "facts," as science, or as common sense knowledge. Two exceptions were an animal protection course and a course in endangered species conservation, where exercises and discussions of values in human-animal relations were carried out. At one animal caretaker school, such sessions were also organized in a social science course for the first time during my field study.

In the more theoretically oriented schools, human-animal education did not seem to be provided on a regular basis, although their natural science courses used animal dissection exercises as a teaching and learning method[1] and elective courses at these schools included horseback riding and hunting/wildlife management. A philosophy course did, however, devote a few lessons to animal ethics issues, primarily oriented around the utilitarian philosophy of Peter Singer.

This book presents "stories" about animals and human-animal relations that took shape in a range of animal-related courses or other activities (such as study visits and school excursions) that were part of the formal curriculum of the schools investigated. However, equally important are those messages and narratives that were produced as part of the *hidden* curriculum (see page 8) in various learning situations. Norms pertaining to meat and dairy production and consumption, commodification of animals and human-animal relations, and various forms of human-animal boundary work are a few examples. Chapters 1-3 describe classroom interaction that lays a foundation for understanding these narratives. These forms of interaction deal to a great extent with identity-shaping processes involving both humans and animals. Chapters 1-3 discuss how animals play an important role in the formation of our individual and collective identities and how they are also ascribed different (and sometimes contradictory) identities by humans.

Chapter 1 deals with conceptualizations of animals in school and the attribution of identity to them. This discussion links to the discourses of the animal body discussed in part II, since, as Desmond (1999) notes, "[a]nimals' identities as authentic representatives of the natural are ultimately presumed to reside in their bodies, in their physical difference from humans" (149). Animals, according to Desmond, are thus seen as fundamentally more embodied than humans, with their identities virtually "inscribed" onto their bodies. This has consequences for what capabilities animals are attributed:

> Animals, as part of nature, are metonymic of the wild; they may possess social organization but are not seen as producing social organizations, cultures, or cultural products. Nor are those organizations seen as subject to historical change and development. (Desmond 1999, 147)

When animals are attributed subjectivity as individuals, for instance, through "anthropomorphic" emphasis of their intelligence or when framed in other "humanized" terms, dimensions of power and control inherent in human-animal relations may be masked, as is often seen in animal shows in zoos or animal theme parks (Desmond 1999). Paradoxically, as chapter 1 will suggest, anthropomorphism also operates to further reinscribe animals' "animality," their fundamental difference from humans.[2]

In chapter 2, the professional role of the animal caretaker is discussed, particularly the socialization the student goes through in her/his vocational education. An intrinsic part of becoming a professional animal caretaker is to learn how to control one's own emotional responses toward animals. To many students this means that they have to *un*learn ways of relating to animals that they are familiar with from their previous, everyday experiences—a process that may give rise to contradictions and conflicts.

Chapter 3 focuses on a radically different part of animal caretaker education: Education for "action competence," that is, ways of improving the situation of animals in human society by various consciousness-raising and action-oriented strategies. The chapter discusses dilemmas teachers face in this context as well as student perspectives on these forms of critical human-animal education.

Notes

1. See Pedersen (2008) for an analysis of animal experimentation in education.

2. The essentializing concept of "animality" does not necessarily describe animals' nature, but configures and consolidates "the exemplarity of the human" (Clark 1997, 182). Birke, Bryld and Lykke (2004) argue that animality, like gender, is complexly constructed and should be seen as a doing or becoming, not an essence.

Chapter 1

Conceptualizing animals

Introduction

A significant element in our sense making of animals is the ways in which we order and categorize them. Ordering can take conceptual as well as physical/spatial forms, and the interplay between these forms influences the very constitution of human-animal relations (Philo & Wilbert 2000). This chapter focuses primarily on conceptual ways of ascribing categories, values, and identities to animals in the school environment and how these attributes interact with the ways animals are represented and understood.

The taxonomical system as a symbol of learning

A primary way of scientifically categorizing animals is by using the taxonomical system, which was an element that appeared as basic knowledge in many animal-related courses during my field study. In classificatory schemes, each thing is separated, identified, delimited, and positioned in its own "proper" conceptual place relative to all other things (Philo & Wilbert 2000). When the objects of classification are animals, the effects of classification fix them "in a series of abstract spaces /.../, which are cleaved apart from the messy time-space contexts, or concrete places, in which these animals actually live out their lives as beings in the world" (Philo & Wilbert 2000, 6-7). Ritvo (1995) describes the production of classification systems as a powerful intellectual act, carried out by an elite of scientists. Both Ritvo (1995) and Foucault (1994) question the presumed scientific objectivity of classification processes:

> Most bodies of material neither define their own boundaries nor provide their own indices, although this taxonomic neutrality may not be obvious to those who use them. Different people identify and structure such bodies of material in different ways, reflecting their various interests, needs, social contexts, and historical experiences. (Ritvo 1995, 419)

> When we establish a considered classification, when we say that a cat and a dog resemble each other less than two greyhounds do, even if both are tame or embalmed, even if both are frenzied, even if both have just broken the water pitcher, what is the ground on which we are able to establish the validity of this classification with complete certainty? (Foucault 1994, xix)

Similarly, Kappeler (1999) describes classification as a political project:

> Classification is neither neutral, being put to political use only "thereafter," nor is it objective: it is itself an act of social and political discrimination and thus the expression of the subjectivity of power. What is said to be a quality of the object is in fact a difference construed in relation to an implicit norm constituted in the classifying subject. (Kappeler 1999, 338)

In animal caretaker programs, the centrality of taxonomy when learning about animals was frequently emphasized. The reasons for this, as explained by teachers, were pragmatic: taxonomy is conceived of as part of the "language of science" that the students must learn in order to find relevant information about animals in literature. Another reason mentioned was that knowledge of taxonomy helps us see how different animal species are related to each other, so that students will be able to conclude how to take care of a particular animal of an unfamiliar species on the basis of its physical resemblance to other animals. Taxonomy is, above all, a way to make clear "what animal we are speaking about" in the classroom. The scheme Kingdom (*Rike*)—Phylum (*Stam*)—Class (*Klass*)—Order (*Ordning*)—Family (*Familj*)—Genus (*Släkte*)—Species (*Art*), in which the Latin or Swedish terms corresponding to particular animal species were inserted, was thus routinely presented to students (either as a full scheme or with a focus on some of its terms) in handouts and on the whiteboard and was also frequently included in various study assignments and tests. Students were encouraged to begin thinking at the most general level and then continue further down the scheme to arrive at the correct classification of the animal. However, students were also presented with classification schemes based on other physically derived principles in order to, according to one teacher, learn "as many ways as possible of naming animals."

The scientific classificatory schemes worked with in the classroom not only function as devices of learning "facts" about animals. They also structure a specific way of thinking about them, of deducing knowledge about a certain individual animal from the characteristics of a generic animal of the same sort. Furthermore, the structures imposed by classificatory schemes are presented as rigid, leaving little room for negotiation or critical inquiry. When filling in the blanks, there seems to be only one correct answer.

The schemes also demarcate boundaries that are not to be transcended. The teacher Rebecka told her colleagues about one of her students who, when he was given the task of filling in the appropriate terms in the classificatory scheme, inserted information on his *own* kinship relations. When the teacher intervened and her instructions were clarified to him, he showed that he was able to insert the "correct" animal data there as well. The rest of this chapter will show that human-animal boundary work in school sometimes encourages continuities between humans and animals, and sometimes emphasizes discontinuities, and animal classificatory schemes may be seen as one element in such boundary work. Furthermore, the schemes not only present systems of meaning demarcating the starting point for where scientific learning about animals necessarily begins (cf. Ritvo 1995), they also become symbols of what ways of *thinking* about animals are considered to be "scientific," and hence, legitimate knowledge (cf. Philo & Wilbert 2000). In this sense, the schemes may be seen as symbolic carriers of a collected body of scientific expert knowledge about animals.

Animals and values

The formal classificatory schemes were not the only approach to categorizing animals in school. Parallel with this conventional form of learning "facts," other processes of conceptualizing animals operated in formal instruction and informal encounters in and outside the classroom. One such process focused on the *value* ascribed to different animals. This issue was discussed particularly during animal ethics seminars in social science classes in one of the animal caretaker programs and in the preceding written student assignments on animal ethics. All these exercises were based on a study material entitled *Animal Ethics* (*Djuretik*; Jordbruksdepartementet 2003).[1] In one of the discussion seminars, the topic of animal intelligence was brought up in relation to value. The students recognized that the character of the relationship between human and animal, rather than the animal's intelligence level, affects the value the animal is ascribed. In the case of "food animals," some emotional distance or detachment must be *created* that allows us to value these animals differently from, for instance, pets, so that we are able to kill and consume them. As one student put it:

> We don't want to get involved with cows and pigs because we eat them. We want them to have lower value so that we don't need to have a bad conscience when [people] eat hamburgers.

However, sharing the same *lifeworld* as an animal means increased possibilities for attachment and hence involvement of other values than otherwise might be the case. As Max (a student in a social science program) put it in an interview with me, animals like dogs and horses "with whom humans sort of can see themselves in the same shared existence" are easier to relate to and will therefore be more highly valued. The classroom discussion referred to above is largely in line with ethnographic research results on farmer-"livestock" relations indicating that certain forms of detachment or similar emotion management processes tend to take place especially when farmers send their animals to slaughter (Falkengren 2005; Wilkie 2005). However, the classroom discussion also revealed that it is important to students to maintain a view that caring about animals is not incompatible with meat consumption habits:

> One student says that it is OK to be an animal friend and to eat meat, it has always been this way, and the animals do it the same way. But the process must be decent (the animals shouldn't suffer). The teacher intervenes: Believing that animals have less value than humans is a precondition for eating meat. It seems as if most people think it's OK that the human being has a higher value, but there are those who think that animals should have the same value as a human being. How do you think that a person like that reasons? Another student in the group remarks that it is possible to like animals and think they have a value even if you eat meat.

The animal's *physical appearance*[2] and *accessibility for cuddling* as well as its *"wildness"* seemed to be highly valued by many students. Ideally, these characteristics would be combined in the same animal. Opportunities to establish physical contact and interaction with a "wild" animal (especially those species denoted by teachers as "charismatic megacarnivores") were often alluded to in zoo advertisements, and in the introduction to her written report on dolphins, a student in an animal caretaker program explains her choice of animal species as follows:

> I want to talk about a wonderful animal, the dolphin. I chose dolphins partly because I think they are so fascinating. I have always been interested in them, but when I was on Bali I had an opportunity to pat them in the

> wild and that was the most awesome [experience] that ever happened to
> me. It was as if something burst [inside me] and everything became clear!
> I love dolphins. As soon as I see them on TV or on film I feel ready to
> cry. They really are the most WONDERFUL animal[s] [in the world].
> (Quoted from student report, my translation)

In the written student assignments on animal ethics in the social science
course in another animal caretaker program, one student added a different
perspective—democracy—to the values discussion:

> If we regard ourselves as having more value than the animals, our society
> would no longer be democratic. Democracy is about allowing everybody to
> think what they want, say what they want and write what they want. Also,
> in a democracy everybody [*illegible*] valuable, which I think also includes
> the animals. /.../ I don't believe in a society that favors a certain "group"
> and regards them as more valuable. (Quoted from student assignment,
> my translation)

This student attempted to place animal ethics in a context of a democratic organization of society. However, the teacher's written comments in the margin
of the student's outline did not focus on her thoughts about the connection
between democracy and animal ethics, but rather on questions familiar from
the classroom discussions and the study material *Animal Ethics* (Jordbruksdepartementet 2003) that was used in this classroom: "Do a human being and
a worm have the same value? Is it OK to eat meat? Why do we kill an animal
that is suffering, but not a human being?"

Although teachers would occasionally join students in their meaning-
making about animals, they would usually keep their focus on quite different
value-related aspects. Biological diversity, whether a (wild) animal species is
regarded as "endangered" or not, and whether it occupies a particularly important niche in the ecosystem, seemed to be central dimensions for teachers
in the animal caretaker program. In an interview, one teacher expressed this
value principle as non-negotiable:

> If you can't see that you must euthanize rabbits so that the ravens can get
> food, or that you must kill rats in order for the snakes to survive, as the
> snakes have a tremendously important niche out in the tropical rainforest,
> then you are not suited to take this education program. Then you should
> take some more time to mature.

Mechanomorphism, zoomorphism, and anthropomorphism

The language used to describe animals can illuminate how animals are conceptualized. This section deals with uses of metaphors and analogies in the description of animals in different learning situations.

Using machine metaphors in relation to animals can be traced back to a Cartesian legacy. Crist (2000) uses the term *mechanomorphism* to describe the technical vocabulary commonly used in classical ethological science,[3] leading to the epistemological representation of animals as "natural objects" (89).[4] Mechanomorphic representations of animals are expressed in ethological writing by both terminology and grammatical constructions. They have the effect of bypassing (or even eradicating) idiosyncrasies, subjectivity, and agency in animals and situating them in a fixed behavioral pattern of innate responses to causal stimuli. Crist (2000) argues that mechanomorphic representations can be both totalizing and deterministic. During my fieldwork, I encountered mechanomorphic expressions in ethology-oriented as well as animal protection classes, school excursions and textbook materials. In photocopied material on ethology, the mechanomorphic language of classical ethology was used, as in this excerpt on "key stimulus":

> Fixed patterns of movement and composite behaviors of which fixed movement patterns are part are in general triggered by very simple stimuli. The trigger mechanism is thereby programmed in such a way so that it reacts to some or a few typical characteristics of the object that triggers a behavior. Such simple stimuli are called key stimuli, since they are thought of as "unlocking and triggering" behaviors, where each key fits only its own specific lock. (*Etologi*, 3, my translation)

In the above passage, external and innate "mechanisms" are agents of action. The animal itself is constructed as an inert object upon or through which forces act (cf. Crist 2000).

In Crist's (2000) analysis, "[t]he stimulus-response connection forms a conceptual home where more explicitly mechanical notions can reside" (96). Classical ethology discourse can thus be thought of as a gateway for animal-machine conceptualizations. In the school contexts I visited, one of the most common mechanomorphic terms used when referring to certain instincts or innate behavior of animals was "programming," but more explicit animal-machine analogies were also expressed. During a school excursion to a nature reserve, our guide at the bird observatory gave us a detailed account of the research work there. In the fieldnote excerpt below he explains how the birds are caught:

> The birds should neither be shocked nor injured, our guide informs us, but adds that they *can't* get shocked and have no thoughts about the future. He exemplifies this by watching TV and other human activities that birds

> are not able to perform. "The crow, of course, has no thoughts at all," the
> guide continues, and shows with the help of a toy bird how it flies into
> the net. /.../ Our guide informs us that the birds are fantastic individuals
> who can convert fat to energy. "Quite simply a flying chemistry lab.
> They change from glutton to aircraft in two, three days /.../ everything
> is programmed."

The expression "flying chemistry labs" to denote birds, as articulated by the
guide above, was substituted by similar wordings for other animal species in
natural science textbook materials: "medical factories" (i.e., genetically manipulated sheep) (Andersson 2003, 74), "bioreactors" and "molecule factories"
(i.e., genetically manipulated farm animals) (Ljunggren et al. 2003, 51, 57).
These conceptualizations may be seen as elements of a discursive practice that
consolidates the technical-objectifying representations of animals already present in classical ethological discourse.

Contrasting with mechanomorphic articulations in school were repeated
conceptual locations of animals in relation to humans, including both anthropomorphic and zoomorphic ideas.[5] In the animal caretaker programs, teaching
strategies in ethology related subject areas seemed to include the human species
as a point of reference, and these strategies generally focused on zoomorphic
aspects, that is, an emphasis on the human being as one among other animal
species. In one school, the common origin of humans and other primates was
emphasized in a basic zoology course, and as part of an ethology course the students in another class were given group work assignments in *human* behavior.
In an introductory ethology class in the other animal caretaker school, zoomorphic conceptualizations were explicitly stipulated not only as an approach
to learning ethological "facts" but also as the "correct" *way of thinking*:

> "You should write like this," says the teacher Robert, writing on the
> whiteboard:
>
> "Never humanize animal behavior, but *animalize* your own!!"
>
> "That means, look at yourselves as the human animal," Robert clarifies.

This zoomorphic statement was a key message in this animal caretaker program and was expected to be embraced by students without further discussion.
It was also reproduced as a matter of fact by students in written social science
assignments on animal ethics (in one case, with direct reference to Robert) and
in an interview I carried out with a third-year student at the school.

Whereas zoomorphic ideas were encouraged or even expected, anthropomorphic expressions were often downplayed, modified, or reformulated in

the mechanomorphic terms of classical ethology. While rejection of anthropomorphism may have a practical purpose of preventing incorrect treatment of animals, there are more dimensions to this phenomenon. In the following fieldnote excerpt from a lesson in animal protection, students had been asked to work in small groups on one of the discussion questions in the material *Animal Ethics* (Jordbruksdepartementet 2003), focusing on differences and similarities between humans and animals:

> The teacher tells her students about experiments aiming to find out whether animals can feel empathy. "Can they?" she asks. "Yes," is heard in unison from the class. One student gives the example of a mother dog who will go to pick up her puppy if it is lying on its own. The teacher starts speaking about *hormones causing mothering behavior*. (My emphasis)

In her analysis of ethological writing, Crist (2000) suggests that there is a tension between the language of ethological science and vernacular, ordinary vocabulary based on different preconceptions of the connection between animal behavior and mental life. Crist proposes that in ethological language, different means of monitoring mental notions, such as on-the-spot translation of "subjective" language into "objective" expressions, are used in order to confirm that technical language "reveals how things really are as opposed to how they only appear to be" (Crist 2000, 119). The example above from a classroom discussion on dog behavior shows a similar tension between the anthropomorphic language used by the student (likely derived from her experiences of dogs in her everyday life) and the mechanomorphic, "professional" linguistic displacement carried out by the teacher.

There were endorsed anthropomorphic conceptualizations of animals in school that emphasized precisely the humanizing of animals that otherwise was implicitly or explicitly to be avoided. During practical training in how to guide visitors in the school's animal facilities, students in one of the animal caretaker programs were encouraged to anthropomorphize animals, although they were not encouraged to do so in other situations. Furthermore, many animals kept at the animal caretaker schools had been given individual—often humanized—names, and a few animals had even been attributed individual biographies, or life histories, that were displayed in written form in appropriate places adjacent to the animal cages or enclosures. According to Phillips (1994), biographies are devices to ascribe unique characteristics to individuals and to situate them in specific historical settings. The biographic narrative also endows coherent meaning to their lives, as well as temporal continuity or cohesiveness. This contrasts sharply with the "scientific" ethological vocabulary that effectively rejects these dimensions (cf. Crist 2000). One of the animal biographies belonged to a cat (cats were the only animals allowed to walk around freely on the school's premises), and another belonged to the ravens.[6] The biographies were detailed, individual narratives about the background and life experiences of these particular animals, which complemented the ordinary information signs containing species-specific facts.

Anthropomorphic tendencies were articulated also in wildlife films (see chapter 4). A few films even seemed to have as their overarching purpose to blur species boundaries and establish the "humanized" character of certain animals. One motive seemed to be to convey a message of the need for the protection of certain animal species, as made clear by a film on the "bush meat" issue shown in an animal protection class, but there were also other dimensions of meaning embedded in anthropomorphic messages. The following passage is from an *Animal Planet* film about simians, shown to the students in a basic zoology class:

> The voice-over speaks about mental capacities in simians and makes a comparison with the development of a human child. /.../ The film shows a young child and an elderly man playing chess. We are told that simians don't play chess, but perhaps they too can imagine how others think.

After repeated messages about the similarities of simians to humans, the film ends with a recasting of the anthropomorphic theme and finds a "unique" characteristic (apart from playing chess) that positions the human subject as distinct from animals: the ability to care about the past and the future.

Species boundaries are thus temporarily blurred but at the same time the arguments presented in favor of human-animal continuities are undermined. There is a paradox present as anthropomorphic messages seem to rely on an implicit consolidation rather than a destabilization of species boundaries (cf. Desmond 1999). If there were no boundaries to transgress, anthropomorphism would lose its meaning.

Conclusions

According to Arluke and Sanders (1996), the classification of animals (or humans) on biological, moral, or social grounds makes it seem "natural" that not everyone or everything is regarded equally. Moreover, classificatory orders are perpetuated by systems of social control (Arluke & Sanders 1996) of which the school may be seen as a part. In the school environment, parallel processes of animal categorization and conceptualization seem to operate and some are explicitly endorsed by formal instruction whereas others are less so. The emphasis on classification schemes in the animal caretaker program may provide for socialization into certain "scientific" views of animals as well as more practical motives such as an understanding of animals' basic needs. The processes of ascribing *value* to animals can either be scientifically framed and motivated, or be located within a social context or within a realm of personal emotions, relations, and morality. I argue that formal, "fact"-based categorizations of animals also are structured by values although these are not explicitly articulated. The following two chapters will further explore what may happen when different ways of making sense of animals collide in school.

There are contradictions and tensions surrounding different "morphisms," or different ways of ascribing identity to animals with humans or machines as analogies, metaphors, or reference points, and these issues were constantly negotiated in school during my field study. Anthropomorphism was probably the most contentious dimension. While anthropomorphism could be used as an argument for animal protection or for rethinking human-animal relations, it also seemed to do a paradoxical job of reasserting the human-animal boundary. Anthropomorphism attributes behaviors or characteristics to animals that are intrinsically coded as human, and Desmond (1999) sees this as a form of *mimicry* that reveals an unbridgeable gap between humans and animals rather than similarities between them. Desmond creates an analogy between anthropomorphism and racial assimilation that can be compared with Bhabha's (1994) analysis of (colonial) mimicry:

> The magical fantasy of anthropomorphism is an extended instance of domination through incorporation /.../. Like the concept of racial assimilation, which is dependent on the idea of different social groupings called races, anthropomorphism makes the partial or temporary erasure of social difference its focus while retaining physical differences (between the category "animal" and the category "human") as the ground of meaning. (Desmond 1999, 210)

> /.../ colonial mimicry is the desire for a reformed, recognizable Other, *as a subject of a difference that is almost the same, but not quite.* Which is to say, that the discourse of mimicry is constructed around an *ambivalence*; in order to be effective, mimicry must continually produce its slippage, its excess, its difference. (Bhabha 1994, 86, emphasis in original)

Despite their different contexts, anthropomorphic messages are, like Bhabha's colonial mimicry, structured around indeterminacy and a "double articulation" (Bhabha 1994, 86), producing (animal) subjects that are *almost* human *but not quite.* Through their negotiation and renegotiation in school, they help keeping the species boundary intact. They are paradoxical (or *ironic*, to use

Bhabha's word) in that they ultimately reinscribe the same boundaries that they are challenging.

Notes

1. The material *Animal Ethics* (*Djuretik*) was produced by the Swedish Ministry of Agriculture and distributed to upper secondary schools all over Sweden. The purpose of the material was, according to the Ministry, to "give a foundation for and inspire discussions on animal ethics" (Jordbruksdepartementet 2003, 32, my translation) in primarily the social sciences, religion, philosophy, and biology.

2. "Cuteness" was attributed to animals frequently and generously by the students in the animal caretaker programs and applied not only to furry, "cuddly" animals, but also to other species such as reptiles.

3. Crist (2000) refers to Konrad Lorenz and Nikolaas Tinbergen as the founders of classical ethology. Classical ethology may be contrasted to new approaches in ethological science, such as "deep ethology" (Bekoff 2002), emphasizing the importance of the scientist caring about the animal and understanding her/his lifeworld and subjective experiences rather than assuming the role of the "objective" observer.

4. See also Haraway's (2004d) cyborg theory for an alternative analysis of animal-machine hybridity and borderland identities.

5. The term anthropomorphism is generally used in a derogatory sense to denote (illegitimate) ways of ascribing human characteristics to animals. Here, I use the terms anthropomorphism and zoomorphism without derogatory connotations to analyze how teaching and learning about animals may be assisted by analogies to human experiences.

6. The ravens seemed to occupy a prominent position at this school. According to the teacher Robert, they constituted an unusual and successful breeding project aiming at the subsequent release of their offspring in the wild. The "story" of the ravens was reproduced in both oral and written narrative accounts during class instruction, in a local newspaper, in an interview, and, as mentioned, on the sign next to the ravens' cage.

Chapter 2

Becoming a "professional" animal caretaker: Emotion management and other forms of socialization

Introduction

Socialization is an identity shaping process with the purpose of fitting the individual to the existing societal order, its culture, and norm system. It generally denotes the long process by which newborn individuals become adult members of their society, and formal education is seen as one agent of socialization (Shor 1992). *Desocialization*, on the other hand, refers to "questioning the social behaviors and experiences in school and daily life that make us into the people we are" (Shor 1992, 114). Desocialization is "a critical rethinking of existing socialization" (117) in the form of an educational counterculture or a form of *unlearning* previously received knowledge. During my field study I found that the process of socialization into the animal caretaker profession that could be observed in school[1] frequently relied on *de*socialization, or unlearning, of students' previous ways of making meaning of animals.[2]

The practical training of handling animals, especially when the training periods were scheduled in the first or second year of study, offered specific insights into students' meaning-making in their close encounters with animals *prior* to having fully adjusted to the expectations of their education. This chapter investigates how students' conceptions of animals are expressed in and formed by direct encounters with them and how these expressions are handled by the school as part of the students' socialization into the animal caretaker profession.

Student-animal interaction

Practical training took place primarily in the schools' animal facilities and during periods of internship outside school (during which I was not present). The purpose of these exercises was to get hands-on experience of working with animals and also to apply and deepen theoretical knowledge learned during classroom instruction. I followed primarily first-year students during their in-house exercises.

The most conspicuous feature of student-animal interaction was the emotive responses from students when handling animals. One of the most frequent expressions of affection was students' responsiveness toward bodily shapes and features of the animals, a phenomenon identified by Myers (1996) as one major parameter organizing child-animal interactions in his ethnographic study of preschoolers.[3] As in Myers's study, touching and petting animals was a much sought-after activity among animal caretaker students, also in situations which did not explicitly require physical handling of the animals (for tasks such as clipping claws).

At one of the schools, the students were asked to cooperatively write a diary during their animal handling classes, specifying which animals they had been working with during the lesson. Diary entries did not only include statements about the animals' conditions, but here and there students had also added comments on whether they had cuddled the animals, and animals who would not let themselves be cuddled were described as "boring." Touching and holding animals (including kissing, stroking, scratching, playing, and talking "baby talk" to them) was commonplace and was also frequently accompanied by comments on the animal's physical appearance (its "cuteness") with a particular focus on details of the animal's body:

> Today, several students picked up and carried animals around (guinea pigs, gerbils, rats) more or less continuously during the entire lesson. The students talk "baby talk" to them and call them "cute." Sometimes they focus on details of the animals' bodies: "Cute nostrils" (a budgerigar), "cute belly" (a frog). A student who doesn't manage to catch and pick up a gerbil says with disappointment, "No gerbils like me today," and after a few moments, "No animals like me today." A few of her classmates hold guinea pigs close to their bodies during almost the entire lesson. They comment on one of the guinea pigs: "She is more social [than the other]," and "Then you feel more appreciated." Another student exclaims that it is boring to be in the bird room. When I ask her why, she replies that you can't cuddle birds; they are not social.

Also nonverbal interaction could express affection, as when the first-year student Jens is introduced to the animals kept at his school:

> Jens picks up the birds' feeding bowls and tries to make them eat from them. Then he opens the door to the cockatoo cage and touches one of the birds carefully with his finger. He touches the bird's leg, beak, and wing. Then he moves on to the smaller parrots, trying to make one of them eat from his hand. Thereafter he goes back to the cockatoo and touches her again. He touches her beak and caresses her feet and claws. From a box full of feathers he picks up a long, red feather and touches it for a while, then returns to the cockatoo and scratches her head, with complete attention directed towards the bird. When she starts climbing on his body Jens gets a little bit scared, and the supervisor intervenes by letting the cockatoo climb over to his own body and then onto a thick rope in the bird's cage.

Although affectionate responses could also include "playful" manipulation of the animal's body or other slightly objectifying behavior, in most student-animal encounters, the animal "other" was related to as a subject with whom at least potential *relationships* could be formed. This is a far cry from the detached, mechanomorphic view of animals in classical ethology as described in chapter 1. With experience, however, students may undergo changes. Jeanette, who graduated from the animal caretaker program six years ago, describes emotional investments in animals as more or less futile:

> You don't get any response from animals, unless you bring them food, but that has nothing to do with emotional responses. To the animals it doesn't matter who takes care of them, providing it is done correctly. It may be cozy having a guinea pig in your lap because it gives you a feeling of warmth, but it could just as well be a warm cushion /.../ It is primarily the internship periods and the work experience that change one's view of animals. You don't project your own feelings onto animals to the same extent anymore. Probably it works in a similar manner for those who work with people. It turns more into technical issues. But some friends from the animal caretaker program have had problems getting over this.

Three years of vocational schooling and six years of work experience have resulted in a considerable difference between Jeanette and the new first-year students with regard to their view of animals and the possibilities of human-animal relationships. According to Jeanette's story, the process of becoming an animal caretaker includes transformations of not only cognitive, but also emotional dimensions. The following section will focus on what previous studies have labeled emotion management strategies (Smith & Kleinman 1989;

Solot & Arluke 1997), which can be employed by the school as part of the socialization into the animal caretaker profession.

The analytic transformation of affection

Students encountered a variety of contradictory messages during their education concerning the level of "acceptability" of emotional bonding in their physical contact with the animals. Whereas schools themselves and/or zoos they worked with could appeal to affectionate dimensions in their public information material in order to attract students and/or visitors, the internal "professional" wisdom in the animal caretaker program accommodated slightly derogatory connotations to what was commonly referred to as "cuddling the animals." The following examples illustrate the contradictory messages of the "public" image, appealing to emotional aspects, and the backstage, "insider" view, focusing on scientific expertise with limited space for expressing emotions (all quotes are my translations):

> The [animal caretaker] education gives you a possibility to access professions where you can feel on a daily basis the happiness of the company of dogs. /.../ During your trainee weeks at a big zoo your close encounters with wild animals will give you knowledge and memories for life. /.../ [Name of school] makes it possible to realize your dreams of working with animals. (Quoted from information booklet from school x)

> Many people think that all you do [here] is pet the animals, but the [study] pace here is tough. (Teacher at school x as quoted in a newspaper article about the school)

> It is not only about caring for an animal, you must also be able to deal with what the animal needs /.../ and have knowledge about a lot of other things. All practical issues must work. It is not only about saying "Oh, how cute!" That is what you spend the least time doing. (Teacher at school y as quoted in a newspaper article about the school)

> Caress a spider, pat a snake or tickle a ray. Mingle with the lemurs or stroll among all the animals of the rainforest. [Name of zoo] brings you into close contact with animals and nature. But no cuddling with crocodiles and cobras of course. (Quoted from zoo information leaflet)

> At the "Farm" you get close to animals, [their] smell and sounds. /.../ You can also jump in the hay, crawl close to the pigs and pat rabbits. (Quoted from zoo information leaflet)

At the annual open house event at one of the animal caretaker schools, students reproduced the "real" zoos' public invitation to make close physical contact with the animals in their information leaflets. However, the "internal" knowledge of proper relations between caretaker and animal was different and it was made clear to the students at this school that engaging in "cuddling" activities with the animals was professionally acceptable if justified by practical tasks. One such task was referred to by the teacher Robert as "inspection." The message of "inspection" was often accompanied by an implicit or explicit expectation that students would unlearn the idea that physical contact with animals is engaged in for the pleasure of it:

> We are watching a film from a zoo. The film shows a close-up of an animal caretaker with his face close to the face of a camel. It almost looks as if his own face is touching the camel's. Robert remarks that "to the uninitiated" it looks as if it is really cozy when the animal caretaker kisses the camel, but "to you as professionals it is inspection," not cozy. You are checking the animal's health. Robert writes on the whiteboard:
>
> "*Inspection of the animals* by close contact with them."
>
> "It is *tremendously* important," he says /.../ The closer the contact the better it is, but the animals must also be allowed to live their wild life.

In this example, the teacher reconfigures the visions of human-animal intimacy that may have attracted many students to the animal caretaker program in the first place.[4] This reconfiguration is achieved by transforming the interaction between caretaker and animal into an analytic event, described in the technical language of "inspection," whose primary purpose is rational rather than emotional. In line with Smith and Kleinman's (1989) study of emotion management strategies in medical school, the training of future animal caretakers may include norms of "affective neutrality" (57), especially in relation to real or imagined physical contact with the animal body that often elicits particular emotional responses among students. Emotion management strategies may be explained by the intention to prevent incorrect treatment of animals; by the intention to prepare the students for a demanding working life where there is likely to be little time available for "cuddling" animals; or by a notion that emotional relations with animal individuals are not fully compatible with a scientific discourse that often values detached "objectivity."

During practical animal care training, emotion management strategies were applied to a lesser extent. Cuddling the animals appeared to be viewed as a more acceptable activity by the supervisors responsible for students' duties at the animal facilities (the supervisors themselves occasionally engaged in such activities), but also in these situations the practical reasons for close physical contact with the animals were often emphasized. At one school, students were encouraged to cuddle the animals for reasons such as stress reduction in animals prior to being handled or just for the pleasure of it in the end of the day if they had completed their duties early. At another school, a teacher described her school's introductory animal handling course as a process of overcoming fear of certain animal species among some students. Her description was supported by a second-year student who told me in an informal conversation that the practical experience of handling animals he had gained during his education had changed his view of both reptiles and rats (animal species that he had previously disliked but now wanted to keep as pets at home).

In theoretical classes, attempts at analytic transformation of students' affection were more obvious and ethology was used as a particularly effective tool for achieving this aim. By encouraging them to analyze their own behavior in ethological terms, students were led to control their own spontaneous feelings about animals. In this manner, ethological science itself was turned into an emotion management strategy (cf. Smith & Kleinman 1989) and a desocialization tool. The following observation was made while watching a zoo film:

> This film sequence is about artificial insemination of pandas. We are shown a successful example of a panda together with her baby. Delighted laughter is heard from the class. The teacher Robert remarks that this is an "aw" animal, referring to the sound the students make when they see the pandas. He says that it is in the students' genes to not be able to resist the cuteness of animal or human babies with flat faces and domed foreheads.

During a lesson on animal instincts the following day, the teacher repeated the message and underscored the correct way of thinking as a professional animal caretaker:

> "And also we humans are exposed to [key stimuli] all the time, but we don't realize it," says the teacher Robert. /.../ We think that little Bambi is infinitely cuter with his flat face and domed forehead, he says, and explains that Disney uses diagrams to measure proportions that evoke feelings of cuteness. A student asks: "Why are we humans so obsessed with physical appearances /.../?" "It is a drive within us /.../" replies Robert, and adds: "And now you are beginning to think the way that real animal caretakers and professionals should think." He turns on the video again. "Look at the upper parts of the nose and forehead," he says when the film shows an adult and a baby baboon. "And the laughter comes

completely naturally," Robert comments on the reactions of his students watching the baby baboon. I agree with you, he says. There is no doubt that we find one cuter than the other.

Analytic transformation of affection into "correct" ethological thinking was also applied in order to neutralize students' tendencies to empathize with prey animals:

> A film sequence shows a baby gazelle being chased by cheetahs. The students express empathy. The teacher comments on his students' reactions: Yes, you start immediately [with your reactions]. It is remarkable. But you don't feel at all sorry for the poor cheetah babies who will starve. /.../ "I am sorry, ladies and gentlemen, you are victims of ethology."

Creation of social ties within the animal caretaker community

The transformation of affection into an analytic event is one form of socialization into the animal caretaker profession. Another form of socialization has to do with the significance and implications of becoming a "professional" and gaining access to a community of animal caretaker colleagues. At one animal caretaker school, it was made clear to the new first-year students from the first orientation day that being part of the program should be considered a privilege and that the mission of future animal caretakers is special, differing from and being more important than other professions:

> The teacher holds a brief introductory speech, emphasizing the students' future responsibility for all living things on earth and the transformation the students will go through from now on during their education. He makes an analogy with the fairytale about Cinderella, where people were transformed into pumpkins at midnight. He says that the school staff are proud. /.../ "You are the future elite in animal care in the world. Never forget that!"

The excellence of the school and its students and their important task of "saving a threatened world" was continuously emphasized during classes, instilling a sense of privilege and pride in students (cf. Smith & Kleinman 1989), and also working as a social glue. Being part of a community of animal caretaker professionals means sharing certain views and experiences that set the animal caretaker profession apart from uninitiated "outsiders":

> You must know your animal so well that you can immediately see how it feels, by looking at only one detail in the animal's appearance or behavior, and other people will [be impressed and] wonder how you can see that. This is the way it will be, says the teacher.

As a way of defining themselves as "professionals," animal caretaker students reproduced the messages that constructed their own learning context as "special" and their knowledge as "insider" knowledge in contrast to the general public. Some of them explained in interviews and conversations with me how they perceived the views, knowledge, and even lifestyles that they had gained during their animal caretaker education, contrasting this both with their previous life before entering the program as well as with their friends outside the program. Occasional clashes in understanding between the different "worlds" they and their friends represent were also mentioned. To these students, like the third-year student Carina below, the animal caretaker program has clearly engendered a sense of belonging to a privileged professional community that is inaccessible or even incomprehensible to others:

> *Pedersen:* Do you think that the view you have of animals here [at your school] is sort of in accordance with [the view] you meet in the rest of society?
>
> *Carina:* No. We learn so much more. /.../ Those [people] in society, [when] you hear other people speaking about [animals], /.../ they don't really know what it is they are talking *about*. We have gone in depth into everything. So we, we think a few steps further ahead. So it's not the same at all.
>
> *Pedersen:* No. Do you often find yourself in discussions with people who don't really know what you are doing here?
>
> *Carina:* Yes, usually, there are a lot of people who are interested in what we do when we work with animals here at the school and so on. And if somebody says something about some animal, and it sort of turns out completely wrong, because you yourself know more. Then you try to explain, and then it gets complicated because they don't understand, and then you try.../.../ Because there is such a big difference when you hear [something] from the outside. It is, yes, such screwy things can come, sort of, from the outside. What *they* think is very correct can be, well, really strange [*laughter*].

A second way of affirming the social ties of the "in-group" was *joking* (cf. Smith & Kleinman 1989). During my field study I found that certain forms of joking occurred both during formal instruction and in less formal situations involving teacher-student interaction such as during study visits. One approach to joking was to accentuate the *hazards* that an animal caretaker may be exposed to as part of the profession. The story about a wolf named Kari who crushed the knee of a caretaker, who was trying to prevent the wolf from threatening visiting children at the zoo, was repeated at least twice by one of the teachers. His remark that the caretaker had almost been given a "punchcard" to the hospital because of her frequent visits to the hospital for her animal bites, gave the story a certain jargon.

Although teachers were often careful not to demonize animals potentially threatening to humans, or exaggerate the risks involved with encounters with such animals, telling adventurous stories was a way of emphasizing that the animal caretaker profession is not for everybody. The teacher John devoted one lesson to telling his zoo management class about his experiences of shark research in the Bahamas, a story replete with dramatic episodes. He also showed the students pictures taken during his stay:

> "I have another shark here that you must see. Here comes one of the most dangerous sharks in the world." John explains how the shark is handled when marked with a data chip by one person holding the shark's head and another holding its tail. John emphasizes again how careful you must be during the procedure and that only the most experienced [researchers] are allowed to hold the shark's head, not just anybody. "So you have to do it quite quickly, because sharks get rather stressed," John says. At the end of the lesson, the students sitting beside me comment to each other that they also want to do this.

Guiding visitors at the animal facilities or at the zoo was a typical situation where the animal caretaker could be exposed to unexpected hazards. During a guiding lesson, the teacher described in detail how once while guiding he was bitten by a large python, but he tried to make a pedagogical point of the incident by letting the visitors look at the marks of the snake's teeth on his hand. One week later in the same class, the teacher encouraged his students to joke about getting their bottoms bitten while standing with their backs against the animal cage during guiding. Clearly, a certain amount of exposure to animal attacks is a way of achieving social prestige in the animal caretaker group.

In an informal interview with the former student Jeanette, she reflected on the particular jargon developed among animal caretakers:

> When you work as an animal caretaker you develop a certain humor that others may not be able to understand, and that may sound cruel and tough to outsiders. Probably all professions develop a certain jargon. I encountered it at all my trainee places. /.../ One example is the animal experimentation community, where there are mice called "popcorn." You genetically modify mice by taking a gene away, and can then follow what happens to another gene. These mice tend more than other mice to be scared and jump when you try to pick them up. Another example

is newborn mouse babies, dead or alive, which are used as food for
other animals. These are called "bubblegum" (*bubbelgum*) or "pinkies"
(*pinkisar*).

This jargon about mice was not restricted to the animal experimentation arena.
It was repeated in the internal school newsletter at Jeanette's school and also
in the other animal caretaker school, when a first-year student under staff supervision was assigned the task of giving a dead baby mouse to a bird spider.
The supervisor explained that these mice are called "pinkies" (*pinkisar*) due
to their pink color. When they start to develop fur they are called "fuzzies"
(*fussisar*), and when they start to jump so that it gets difficult to catch them
they are called "popcorn."

Joking (sometimes as part of potentially dangerous shared experiences),
together with elevating the special knowledge and insights of the animal caretaker above other professions (and especially above the general public), are two
elements in the formation of boundaries around the professional group identity
in the animal caretaker program.

Conclusions

Patterns of spontaneous student-animal interaction in the early phases of
animal caretaker training derive from experiences of and views of animals
acquired by students as non-professionals, prior to their entering vocational
school. Their ways of relating to animals at this time are still largely emotion-
ally driven and may clash with expected "professional" behavior, which often
relies on rationality and affective neutrality for its credibility.

The different dimensions of socialization described in this chapter—
emotion management strategies and various ways of creating a feeling of "we-
ness" by forming social ties within the group—work together to help students
collectively define the value of shared experiences (real or imagined) within a
common frame of reference, and develop a sense of self as a professional animal
caretaker from whom certain views and behaviors are expected, whereas others
are considered less appropriate. In their study of medical school, Smith and
Kleinman (1989) propose that the professional culture that informs teaching
includes a hidden curriculum where not only skills and knowledge, but also
emotive responses and ways of thinking become professionalized. The sense
of privilege in becoming a "real" professional who knows how to take proper
care of animals becomes a motivating force among students, but as animal
caretaker novices, their immediate responses (often including affection, but
in some cases also fear or repulsion) to the physical presence of animals may,

at least at the beginning of their education, compete with the more rational approaches expected of them. Affectionate responses are not entirely discouraged by the school, but students are expected to learn how to control their own responses and this is part of a *de*socialization process that the socialization to the animal caretaker profession relies on (although the schools differed as to how much they focused on this aspect). This desocialization process may have pragmatic grounds such as allowing animals to keep their natural behavior and focusing attention on the animals' health condition rather than on their "cuteness," but it also produces ambiguities. The contrast between encouraging the general public to "cuddle" animals for the pleasure of it, compared to "backstage" messages of the primacy of scientific rationales, constitutes a double articulation of the legitimacy of such behavior and at the same time reinscribes the differences between the "professional" and the "uninitiated."

Notes

1 Students' professional identities as animal caretakers are formed over time during all phases of their vocational education and work experience, and the classroom observations presented in this study offer only a partial view of the socialization process.

2 This use of the concept of desocialization differs from the common understanding of the term, denoting a counterhegemonic context or purpose.

3 Although my adolescent informants belonged to a different age group, Myers's (1996) analysis corresponds with my findings on this point.

4 One student told me that many students in the program choose to become caretakers or assistants instead of veterinarians in order to have more contact with the animals.

Chapter 3

Education for action and the teacher role

Introduction

How teachers view their assignments as educators of human-animal relations, and how they express these views in the classroom, were questions of particular interest to me during my field study. Chapters 1 and 2 outlined some general strategies for the "professionalization of emotions" in students (Smith & Kleinman 1989) that largely work to consolidate and reproduce "rational," detached, and scientific human-animal relations conforming with a classical ethological view of animals. This chapter will focus on a radically different dimension of teaching human-animal relations: Teaching as a tool for *action* in order to challenge the status quo and change the position of animals in human society.

In the field of environmental education, Jensen and Schnack (1994) have interpreted action as activities addressing solutions to environmental problems that are being worked on in school and decided on by those carrying out the action. Action *competence* may be defined as an ability to work for changes on the level of individual lifestyle, but also "to be able to collaborate with other people on changing collective conditions for everyday life" and to engage in "responsible actions and counter-actions for a more humane world" (Schnack 1994, 186, 190). The idea of action competence is thus closely associated with student empowerment and involvement.

Linking critical pedagogy with environmental education, Fien (1994) emphasizes three key notions in what he terms "education *for* the environment": critical thinking, values education (i.e., development of an environmental ethic), and political literacy (i.e., active participation in political systems of power and decision making). Instead of "political literacy," Selby (1995) speaks in broader terms about "involvement literacy," which he defines as follows:

> [Involvement literacy] encompasses the exploration and evaluation of the range of avenues and strategies open to those who wish to effect change. It calls for mature reflection upon the effectiveness, ethics, limitations, pitfalls and ramifications of different types of action and upon the rights and responsibilities of both the change agent and those who will be caught up in the change process. (Selby 1995, 317)

To attempt to uncover some meanings that action competence in human-animal education may involve, I will begin by outlining teachers' own descriptions of their role as (critical) educators of animal-related issues and then review actual teaching approaches to action competence as observed in the classroom. Finally, I will include student voices to give their views as recipients of teaching for social change.

Teachers' views

The ideal of "neutrality"

Teachers differed significantly in the way they presented their approaches to their work, their subject areas, and their aims as educators. Whereas most teachers and school leaders introduced themselves to me by giving their educational background and professional experience, Gunilla, who teaches animal protection and animal health care related subjects, also emphasized her animal activist background. However, she repeatedly expressed concern that her personal standpoints would influence her students and has developed teaching strategies in order to avoid this. Based on her teaching experience, Gunilla has found ways of balancing the conflict she feels between her personal standpoints, which (in her view) deviate from dominant human-animal discourses in society, and the requirement to maintain a "neutral" position in the classroom. One strategy is to show the students "different perspectives":

> Whatever issue we are discussing, if we are talking about hunting or we are talking about breeding cows in order to eat them, if I *am* a farmer living in the countryside or if I live in the city and never have been in the countryside, you twist and turn the issue *all* the time, in all subjects, and must see it from everybody's perspective. And *that* is so good for them [the students], as they are so used to seeing black or white, black or white, at their age.

Gunilla encourages her students to valorize arguments and materials from different animal-related stakeholders in society in order to arrive at independent standpoints, but she still feels concerned that her articulation of her own personal views on human-animal relations in the classroom poses a potential indoctrination problem in her role as a teacher. She has solved this dilemma by refraining from giving her own view until the end of the class:

> They [the students] read like a *barometer* how I appear to have taken a stance for thinking in this way or that way. Then at some point, at last of course I tell them my point of view, but that must come at the *end*, *my* personal, because I don't have to *hide* it.

Sofie, one of Gunilla's colleagues, also expressed the importance of showing the students different perspectives, making them realize that people have different views and values, and letting them discuss and justify their arguments. When I asked Sofie what she sees as most difficult when teaching about animal protection issues, she replied that the most difficult thing is to be neutral. Prior to each lesson she really tries to prepare herself by studying "both sides" of the issue she will deal with in class. Like Gunilla, Sofie says that many students see things in "black and white," especially when it comes to animal issues.

Some teachers, on the other hand, did not stress neutrality but were very clear about the school having a responsibility to convey certain views of human-animal relations. One teacher explained that "We *must* educate disciples who will go out in the world and preach." Another teacher stated that the school should "convey the view [of animals] that we want to prevail in our society." Yet another teacher explained that the school's role regarding animal ethics is to show respect toward animals while also clarifying that "there is a difference between human beings and animals, what the difference is, and that they [the students] can see this difference."

Teaching action competence

While "neutrality" was a concern for teachers with a critical view of human-animal relations, there was still space for discussing action-oriented activities in their classrooms. Gunilla frames her approach as part of her ambition to teach animal protection issues in a coherent way:

> I think that it is important that they [the students] *understand* this too, how things hang together and that you as an individual [can say that], sort of, "I think like this, I have an opinion, I, I *can* take part in *influencing* this."

Gunilla discusses with her students what ways to choose if you want to do something for the animals. Her main point in these discussions is that there are many things to do that fall between the long process of political work (which, Gunilla remarks, may seem insurmountable to a seventeen-year-old) and making attacks. Gunilla says that her discussions with her students will have a domino effect since the students will discuss with their families and friends, who, in turn, will discuss with others. When she disseminates knowledge to her students about things important to know in one's daily life, they may spread this knowledge to others. One example is that they may start buying organically produced products.

At the theoretical programs, the social science teachers Inga and Eric both refer to the students' desire to influence society as an inspiration for their teaching approaches when the situation of animals in society is brought up in the classroom:

> The issues often come up when we talk about the EU and EU politics… animal transport and BSE and…then there are lively discussions. It's the same when animals are used in experiments. It comes up as societal issues in social science classes. And…then there are lively discussions. How to act in order to influence…minks held in captivity and if you can release minks, what the consequences are. So there are lively discussions. /…/ At times, they [the students] can be very *upset* about this, do we *have* to treat [the animals] during *cosmetics* testing, and what do they *do* to the animals [in] animal experiments. *Those* initiatives have been brought up. They want to discuss this and want to influence. (Inga)

> I speak about the societal perspective in the sense that you should know who, so to say, has responsibility for the issues. And also how it works to change…this. In order to sort of get some understanding that issues can be complex and difficult you must be able to shed light [?] on a discussion. /…/ You should know who has the responsibility for different issues that relate to animal rights. I usually say to the students, you must be able to find the right tree to bark up. (Eric)

Gunilla, however, has done more than just help her students "find the right tree to bark up." She has encouraged activism among her students, and in one of her classes, activism became a big issue. Students started disseminating flyers and posting protest lists, but Gunilla found that students who did not want to get involved in that way risked getting singled out by their classmates. Consequently, she has changed her approach and will not give her students concrete tools for taking action anymore since she is afraid that they may get the idea that activism is part of the course grading system. Instead, she refers students, who want to take action, to the NGO Animal Rights Sweden. Gunilla says that she has probably recruited a significant number of students to this organization.

Another activity that Gunilla has stopped doing with her classes is taking them on study visits to places such as slaughterhouses. She explains the reasons for this as follows:

> There is no reason to take students there because they are already upset and on their way to becoming vegetarians anyhow, if I didn't *curb* them. And if I took them to a slaughterhouse, there is *nobody* who would eat meat after that, at least not for a month, then maybe they will have forgotten. /.../ I feel that, my students who are so sensitive, we watch films, quite a lot of films in the course and I warn and warn prior to [watching], and even then they just sit like this, crying and are unable to eat. So, I changed my approach a lot. There is no reason to *show* things that produce *such* terrible reactions.

Still, Gunilla supports her students' activist initiatives wholeheartedly. She mentions as an example when students, after an animal protection lesson that dealt with the production of dog and cat fur products, wanted to go out in senior compulsory school classrooms and talk about this particular issue. But while encouraging activism, she also emphasizes the value of taking even small steps in a positive direction. Trying to counterbalance the tendency she sees among students to see things in "black and white," she wants to make them feel proud if they manage to make just *one* small change in their daily life (such as persuading their families to buy organically instead of conventionally produced milk).

When asking her if she has ever had comments from her students' parents regarding her way of teaching to achieve social change, Gunilla says that this has never happened. Before the start of the animal protection course, she usually informs the parents of the first-year students about the course, saying that it will stir up a lot of emotions, and that the parents should be prepared to hear their children's critical comments (for instance, against fur coats) at the kitchen table. She also tells the parents that she presents facts and perspectives that we would otherwise choose not to see.

Action competence in the classroom: The fur issue

In the animal protection classroom, one example that was dealt with in an explicitly critical manner was the fur issue. Lessons on mink fur production alternated between the teacher Gunilla's outline of facts about the species and its living conditions in the wild as opposed to in the fur farm and critical comments and discussions on mink farming and trapping of wild minks.

> Gunilla draws a simple sketch on the whiteboard illustrating how a trapper might move in the forest, to show how long time it can take before the traps are emptied. She says that the trapped animals often get completely desperate in the meantime. She refers to films available at Animal Rights Sweden, but says that these are so horrid that she has stopped watching them. Gunilla talks about the injuries the animals get from the traps and that they could be stuck in a trap for several days. She also talks about the different ways in which the animals die in the traps. "Did you read about this guy who sawed his own arm off with a nail file?" she asks her students. /.../ Gunilla encourages her students to imagine what it would feel like. Then she reads aloud from a text that trappers often kick or beat the animals to death in order to avoid damaging the pelts. She talks about a special type of trap in which the animals get stuck with a broken back or internal injuries. She draws a simple sketch of such a trap on the whiteboard.

Gunilla's teaching strategy is to appeal to her students' empathy with the trapped animals, and she asks them to imagine how they would feel if they were in the animal's situation. But Gunilla also links this approach to possible ways of taking action for the animals, such as critical consumer activism, and gives an example when she herself has used this possibility. The radical action of releasing trapped animals is, however, a sensitive issue in the classroom:

> Gunilla: "Now we will talk about something called *trash animals*." She explains that "trash animals" are "wrong" animals that end up in the traps and says that these animals are often just left behind with their injuries. This applies also to endangered species, which is one reason for banning traps. Another reason is that traps are cruel. She asks her students to underline in their handout that many endangered species get stuck in the traps. One student asks if one is allowed to save a [trapped] animal that one finds in the forest. Gunilla replies that it is a difficult question. The trapper would get very angry if he saw you.

Gunilla concludes the trapping discussion by saying that Animal Rights Sweden has a lot of information on the fur issue on their Web site. A written test at the end of the semester included questions about how animals react when trapped, stereotypical behavior in caged fur animals, how fur animals suffer in cages considering their natural needs, and how minks are slaughtered. Further underscoring the criticism against fur was a piece of news about the majority opinion against fur farms from Animal Rights Sweden's Web site, copied into the internal newsletter at Gunilla's school at the end of the year.

At the other schools I visited, none of the lessons I observed dealt with action-oriented education similar to the lessons described above. One exception was a class on endangered species, during which commercial fishing was discussed:

> The teacher Sten mentions that he will order a brochure from the WWF that gives information about what sorts of fish to avoid buying if you want to be a conscious consumer. Sten tells his students how he has tried to influence the school canteen on this issue. But he says that he does not want to impose anything on anybody, it is up to each and everyone to decide. He says that he himself likes cod very much.

Like Gunilla, Sten gives himself as an example of the possibility to take action to achieve change, but his statement also reflects a concern about "neutrality" as a teacher and his action-oriented approach is softened accordingly.

Action-oriented approaches in learning materials were difficult to find but in the "Economy" chapter of a social science textbook, a section on consumer issues deals with consumer power:

> /.../ Do we have a possibility to influence the supply [of products] in the shops? Yes, for instance, by refraining from buying products that do not satisfy the demands we make.
>
> If you think that the animals are not treated in a good way, you can simply stop buying meat and leather. If you do not like child labor, you can make a choice by refraining from buying clothes produced by the hands of children. If you want to care about the environment, you can make sure that you buy products that are produced in an environmentally friendly way and do not generate a lot of unnecessary waste.
>
> If there are many people who actively make a choice, it will force the companies to improve the way animals are handled, work against child labor and take the environment into consideration. As a consumer you can use your money to gain power. Other possibilities are trying to influence other people, protesting against a certain company that you think is doing wrong and helping form public opinion (influencing the view of the public). /.../ (Cronlund 2003, 118, my translation)

Generally, however, I found that explicit encouragement of action was rare in both classrooms and in learning materials. The animal protection course was an exception. The following section highlights perspectives of students who have participated in that course.

Students' views

How does it feel to be a student in a critical educator's classroom? This section will focus on the viewpoints of two students: the second-year student Lisa and the first-year student Sara.

In an interview with Lisa, she let me know that the animal caretaker program, and especially the animal protection course, had made a big impact on her. When asked whether she has changed her view on animals since she had begun the program, she replied "*Very* much." Previously, she had not been aware of environmental problems and the way animals are treated in society, but now things are different:

> I didn't know what it looked like in the rest of the world…endangered species, didn't know what animal transportation looked like, and things like that. And that has *really* opened my eyes [*laughter*]. "We must buy this, we can't buy that. I will *not* go to McDonald's. I will… skip that," and "Hey, daddy, don't buy that sausage," and things like that. I really have…learnt. /…/

Lisa explains that her involvement comes from a sense of personal responsibility, evoked by her education, and describes the powerful emotional impact of the animal protection course:

> /…/ and sometimes I even feel like I want to cry, because when one sees something with one's own eyes, then one understands. And then, actually, I feel *bad* because then I can't *walk around* in a shop and have the nerve to, [*Lisa quoting herself*] "Right, look at all the tasty meat." Then there is a feeling of disgust. Automatically, one starts reflecting. /…/

Lisa places particular emphasis on her relations with her family in her process of changed awareness. She has not only influenced her parents' and neighbors' consumption patterns in a more environmentally and animal friendly direction, but she has also educated school children about animal issues with the help of her mother, a compulsory school teacher. Lisa mentions that now she can even imagine going back to her previous school to inform them about animal issues:

> I and my friends brought it up, but then it flopped, but at that time we thought that we had sort of enough competence to be able to, it felt as if I would be able to go back to my old school maybe. Going around to those [pupils] above all of one's own age and the age below, to begin with, and show a film and give information. Tell them what it looks like today. Because I think that there are so many people who don't know about animal ethics. And then…regulations and such things and…now there

are so many people walking around in Canada Goose jackets. With some arctic fox attached to the collar. And then you can show a film, they might take it as an accusation, but…no, they will just have to take it.

Lisa sees the idea of going to schools (and other workplaces) to give information as a way of building up public opinion (or, in her own words, to "bring more people along"). She also feels that she and her classmates have enough support from their present school to be able to do this.

Lisa describes certain issues as easier to act against than others. She feels that selling trophy hunting travel packages at travel agencies would be difficult to stop, whereas animal transport and the fur industry are problems that feel "closer" to her and thus possible to act against by convincing people around her to change their consumption patterns. Lisa describes her involvement as a way of achieving step-by-step improvements for animals in society rather than as an expression of far-reaching animal rights ideas, and is not in principle against the continued use of animals in areas such as hunting, meat production, and animal experimentation.

Whereas Lisa attributes her involvement entirely to her education and especially the animal protection course, this is not the case with Sara. Sara is a first-year student at Lisa's school and a vegan; in contrast to Lisa, she has previous experiences from hanging around with radical, left-wing activists when she began upper secondary school. With her friends, she has been sitting in animal rights cafés (according to Sara, places that do "ordinary" café business but have animal rights activities behind the scene), and Sara has learned about animal issues from them. Her present classmates are not part of this context. Sara describes in detail her activist past involving taking part in masked demonstrations (the mask, she explained, would protect her from being identified by Nazis), but a personal conflict made her lose interest in these activities, and she is not politically active anymore.

Although Sara attributes everything she learned about animal issues to her friends outside school, she also thinks that the animal protection course has contributed by giving her an insight into what is behind the issues:

> It feels good that the teacher dares to show the truth. [The teacher] brings up important issues. She is not entirely unbiased, but can bring up arguments from both sides [and] discuss [them]. There is a free flow of thoughts.

Sara thinks that it is good when teachers do not take up a position. They should be unbiased and be able to "talk with themselves." Sara hates it when people try to convert her. She feels that many teachers try to do that, try to brainwash her, saying that her viewpoint is wrong. Sara says that a few other students have similar experiences. She believes that the teachers feel that they are being accused and that their behavior is a way of protecting themselves.

In my informal interview with Sara, I asked her how she would organize a course in animal protection/animal ethics/animal rights if she were a teacher teaching a group of students of her own age. I expected her reply to somehow reflect her activist past, but instead she stayed close to the ideals she had just described about the "unbiased" educator:

> I would get information from the slaughter industry and from animal rights organizations and make students compare their materials and look at what is good and what is bad. They would make written reports on some animal, how it is treated in different situations such as at the slaughterhouse. Would the animal make it without the human being, and does it benefit society if we preserve them/eat them/don't eat them? I would also give the class a test by dividing it into two groups, with one group acting as if they were militant animal rights activists, and the other group arguing in favor of killing animals in, for instance, research. They would look for pros and cons on both sides, and have a discussion without trying to convert each other. I would also arrange study visits to slaughterhouses and animal experiment institutions, bring an animal rights organization to these places and start a discussion. The students should be allowed to think freely, *entirely* by themselves, in order to get them thinking about these things. The course should be a basis for the students arriving at whatever viewpoint they want. It shouldn't be a long course, perhaps some thematic arrangement for a month or so. If it is too long, it will get off track and the students will start thinking like their classmates. The entire thing should be like an exercise. After a while you become influenced, even if it [the course] is unbiased.

With this description of her ideal animal ethics course, Sara largely mirrors the teaching strategies outlined by her teacher Gunilla, seeking to show her students "different perspectives," and, above all, to be unbiased and "neutral." Although activism has apparently played a significant role in the development of Sara's knowledge about animal issues, she appears to draw a clear line between life in and outside school, which she sees as two different contexts.

The animal caretaker program may to some extent seek to foster action competence in students, but these ambitions risk being neutralized not only within the school, but above all afterwards when students enter their professions. Jeanette, who graduated from Lisa's and Sara's school six years ago, said in an interview that experiences from her trainee periods and working life have changed her view of animals. Just after graduation, she wanted to *act* on behalf of the animals and "rescue" them. These ideas in part disappeared during her trainee periods but above all as she gained work experience, and she no longer believes that animals are always better off in nature than in captivity.

Conclusions

To the extent that it is possible to talk about action competence in human-animal education, action competence seems to be a complex approach to teaching that is not free of tensions. Despite these tensions, the empirical materials presented in this chapter suggest that there is space for critical, action-oriented education in some classrooms. This could include activities addressing changes on the level of individual lifestyle or on the level of societal/political structure as seen, for instance, in the teaching about fur production and consumption issues. One aim seems to be to create synergy effects that will ultimately lead to positive changes in the lives of animals.

One source of concern in the critical human-animal education classroom is the ideal of "neutrality." Why is there such a focus on neutrality among teachers and students whose personal views on human-animal relations seem anything but neutral? In Sara's case, she has negative experiences of teachers trying to "convert" her to a way of thinking considered more acceptable in mainstream society, which may explain why she now appreciates what she calls "unbiased" teaching. Similarly, her teacher Gunilla has realized how easily students adopt their teacher's point of view and is thus careful about how she expresses her personal values in class. Fien (1994) discusses the ideological ends served by values pluralism and claims of neutrality and suggests that these ideals originate from a liberal orientation to education. The liberal position holds that students should be taught about the range of values and how to clarify their own standpoint in relation to them, but fails to acknowledge that school curricula and practices reproduce dominant patterns of power and control in society. This position overlooks the hidden curriculum of the values that underlie the case for neutrality. I would like to add that it is primarily underrepresented standpoints that risk being conceived of as "biased." While critical educators more or less seem to feel that they are expected not to favor any particular perspective, teachers representing more dominant views seem more likely to take the legitimacy of these views for granted, as well as the need to mediate them in the classroom.

Fien (1994) argues that the study of controversial issues in environmental education is a political exercise and should be openly acknowledged as such, with teachers' and students' commitments being shared and critical thinking and acting skills encouraged, but Shor (1992) points to a necessary delimitation:

"Students cannot be commanded to take action and cannot be graded on their consciousness. They can only be presented with critical problems and invited to think and act on them." (197) To this I would add the importance of situating the problems in a social, political, and historical context since, without a critical analysis of the vested interests and forces behind the situation of animals in society, students are withheld central explanatory dimensions.

PART II

Educational encounters with animal practices

The previous chapters have shown that education involving human–animal relations can be based on textual or verbal narratives and involve both visual and physical encounters with animals (living or dead). The chapters that follow discuss how these different modes of teaching and learning may take shape in school in relation to a range of animal practices and institutions, including zoos, wildlife watching, animal agriculture, and hunting.

Visual observation of animals and their behavior is often emphasized in science education as an important way of learning about them. There are, however, reasons for questioning the idea of observing animals as an "innocent" and unproblematic act. Visualizing practices may require arrangements involving direct coercion, harm, or abuse of animals, but may also include more subtle forms of violence. In either case, the act of viewing may assign and reinforce certain social positions to animals and contribute to legitimate their status as objects. For instance, reliance on sophisticated visualizing technologies and arrangements in areas such as zoo displays and wildlife filmmaking produces increasingly intimate exposures of animals' daily lives and even their bodily interior (Willis 1999; Chris 2006), and in animal research laboratories, instruments of visualization that enhance and extend the limits of observation are used (Shapiro 2002). The varied "apparatuses of visual production" (Haraway 1991, 195) not only structure relations between the observer and the observed, they can even blur the boundary between the instrument and the observed object (for instance, when a "lab animal" is chronically implanted with an electrode connected to a machine that records and displays responses) (Shapiro 2002).

In an outline of visual culture, Hooper-Greenhill (2001) describes vision as a social practice, raising questions such as what is made visible, who sees what, and how seeing is interrelated with knowing and power. The relationship between vision, knowledge, and power has also been analyzed by Berger (1980), who notes that animals are always the observed and the objects of our knowledge, and that the knowledge we gain when observing animals becomes an index of our power over them, further separating us from them. The one who is observing is thus the privileged eye, the bearer of reason, the author, the knower (Anderson 1998). Desmond (1999) has framed this structure of power hierarchies implicit in viewing as a "politics of vision" (155) that makes it possible to commodify, elaborate, and sell public displays of how animal (and some categories of human) bodies look, what they do, and where they do it.

There are several parameters that structure our viewing of animals, and one parameter concerns the situations or venues in which viewing takes place (Desmond 1999). The production, crossing, and maintenance of borders between the physical spaces assigned to humans and animals, but also between human and animal identities, is a central dimension of meaning-making in the process of viewing animals (Desmond 1999). According to Desmond, the animal's bodily difference is the foundation from which our viewing of them gains meaning, and the simultaneous confusion and reinscription of species boundaries is central to this meaning-making process. Our visual "consumption of radical bodily difference" (Desmond 1999, 144) can be anthropomorphically framed and recoded into similarities with human physical and behavioral traits, but this recoding ultimately functions to reassert the human-animal species boundary. As Desmond notes, anything the animal does eventually reaffirms our concept of it *as* an animal "other," and the same logic may be applied when the objects of viewing are *human* "others" in, for instance, "exotic" tourist venues.

The crossing of barriers between "us" and "them" is a theme that recurs in Franklin's (1999) analysis. He uses the term "the zoological gaze" to describe the act of viewing animals as a social, cultural, and historically specific process that has been organized and reorganized over time through changing institutions and social practices: from anthropocentric visual consumption of animals as vehicles for recreation and entertainment in the early twentieth century to a more zoocentric or ecologistic form of zoological gaze concerned with species and habitat preservation from the late 1960s. According to Franklin, we are now experiencing a postmodern zoological gaze by which the human-animal species barrier is repeatedly breached and confused by inviting feelings of intense involvement with the animals' world. During my own field studies,

I could trace elements of all three forms of a zoological gaze as identified by Franklin, although not as representations of clearly demarcated historical periods, but as simultaneously co-occurring and intertwined dimensions.

The zoological gaze not only shapes, frames, and "fixes" animals in the act of viewing, but also expresses their more general objectification under the logic of dominant societal and cultural regimes. In these processes of "fixing" animals into given conceptions, Baker (2001) writes that human culture may render even animals, which are fully exposed to our view, effectively *in*visible— that is, either seen as mere vehicles for the transmission of symbolic meaning or drained of any significance whatsoever (cf. Berger 1980). The following chapter will explore these processes, as well as processes by which the visibility of animals is *reclaimed* in learning situations.

Viewing is not, however, always a static, one-dimensional process, and the ways we structure our viewing of animals do not necessarily imply that, as Berger (1980) argues, "[t]he fact that they can observe us has lost all significance" (14). Nor do I fully agree with Haraway's (2004a) claim that to be the object of vision is to be evacuated of agency. Rather, the desire for interaction, to get a *response* from the animal observed, was a driving force in many students' visual involvement with animals during my field study. But, again referring to Desmond (1999), this desire for interspecies interaction may include an idea of both the crossing of a barrier and its simultaneous reassertion in order for the imagined intimacy to be meaningful.

Student encounters with animals can also be of a physical character. These encounters are often structured by the general status of the animal body as accessible for manipulation and control, rather than as subjected to the animal's own integrity. As will be demonstrated throughout the following chapters, this understanding of the animal body as open to human use is in many cases both controversial and contested, not least in school, and may be viewed as a site of struggle between competing discourses and systems of meaning.

Many contexts of human-animal encounter and use seem to entail an idea that animals *are* their biological-material bodies, entrenched within a realm of ahistorical biological fixity (Birke 1994). Their cultural meaning *is* as bodies, not as selves (Birke & Parisi 1999). Animal bodies are conceptualized as commodities, production units, "renewable" natural resources, trophies, and as "models" for various human diseases. The reduction of the individual being to her/his biological functions is a form of subordination that animals throughout history have shared with categories of "otherized" humans.

To conceptualize animal (and human) bodies beyond a mere collection of biological functions and processes, bodies may be seen as surfaces that can be coded, marked, or inscribed with various ethically and socially charged meanings (Birke 1994; Elder, Wolch & Emel 1998; Philo & Wilbert 2000; Twine 2001), but also as active agents engaging with social inscriptions, for instance, when a "lab rat's" biting and squealing disrupts the data produced from the experiment (Birke, Bryld & Lykke 2004).

Desmond (1999) remarks that both human and animal bodies function as material signs for categories such as gender, race, cultural identity, and species. This means that (perceptible) bodily differences are seen as meaningful in themselves and are "marked, calibrated, measured, and mobilized politically to naturalize various social relations" (xxiv). In this manner, the body functions epistemologically to anchor paradigms of social difference and classifications as well as certain ideological formulations. The power of this conception of the body is reflected by human and non-human typologies and taxonomies of which bodily difference is a basis (Desmond 1999).

Animal bodies have been disciplined, standardized, and put to use in animal agriculture, biotechnology, and entertainment industries. In the industrial manufacture of animal bodies, some bodily characteristics and behaviors are seen as non-profitable or otherwise undesirable and simply done away with, whereas others are enhanced or (if not there from the start) artificially produced. In these ways, animal bodies are moulded and incorporated into human-controlled enterprises (Noske 1997). As Desmond (1999) remarks, it is imperative to uncover the various meanings of physical presence and how they operate within systems of social differentiation, legitimate exploitation, and obscure the complexities of its historical origins that have rationalized human and animal oppression with a similar logic.

In human-animal interaction and practices, the act of viewing animals and the act of handling and using their bodies are often closely interlinked, and both modes of relating to animals are integrated parts of the experience and meaning we create from them. As will be demonstrated throughout the following chapters, the school is an arena where significant implications of these meaning-making processes emerge. Chapter 4 explores how animals are used as visual "tools" in education and the power dimensions implicated in this use. Chapter 5 focuses on the school's role in the globalized "animal economy," and in chapter 6, classroom negotiations around the killing of animals are discussed.

Chapter 4

Education, animals, and visual power arrangements

Introduction

During encounters with zoos and wildlife watching activities on film and in nature, students' approaches to watching animals were structured by the formal and informal arrangements of the various learning situations. In each case, different modes, actors, and artefacts were present as mediators of knowledge about animals; such as teachers, guides and other professionals, filmmakers, voice-overs, written materials, visual equipment, and the built or natural environment. The interaction between these mediators and the students helped shaping the human-animal relations that emerged from the visual encounters with animals as part of the school curriculum. This chapter presents examples from teaching and learning activities connected to zoos and watching wildlife. It explores how multiple, and often contradictory, meanings about animals and human-animal relations are produced and negotiated in each context.

The zoo as a pedagogical "tool"?

The zoo has been described as a place where animals are gathered, confined and (re-) presented to the public. They are not there as individual, subjective beings, but as signifiers of their species, and are assumed to display species-typical behavior (Anderson 1998). They are also categorized and displayed in specific ways so as to produce certain pedagogical and entertainment-related outcomes (Willis 1999). Many analyses of zoos from educational perspectives focus on what is perceived to be their educational benefits, assuming that they replicate a "true" representation of "nature." The animals confined there are reduced to being educational instruments presenting themselves to the learner. As Milson (1990) has expressed it, zoos, aquariums, and museums can be "a living laboratory" for school children, and he describes the zoo as a place where children can observe "the physical characteristics, behavior, adaptations, habitats, diets, and locomotion methods of animals" (523-24):

> Museums, zoos, and aquariums have always held great potential for teaching and learning. They are the perfect "tool" for supplementing classwork with artifacts, works of art, fossils, historic relics and collections of almost every kind. They show the "real thing," instead of the written description that children receive in a textbook. (Milson 1990, 521)

This view fails to take into consideration, and to problematize, the multiple meanings performed by the zoo. Anderson (1998) provides a perspective on the zoo that differs from Milson's (1990) above. According to Anderson (1998), zoos in the West historically evolved out of a desire to classify and control the non-human world. In her analysis, she relates the human-nature relations mirrored by the zoo to feminist and postcolonial critiques of Western science and philosophy. Acampora (2005) even speaks about zoos as pornographic in their way of overexposing their subjects. In the process of marketing and consumption of the animals' visibility, they are degraded or marginalized.

As suggested in the background preceding this chapter, the act of viewing is not innocent, especially when institutionalized. Foucault (1995) compares Bentham's *Panopticon*—an architectural blueprint for the prison, providing an environment for ultimate surveillance—with the menagerie, a private collection of caged animals that formed the early version of the zoo:

> At the center was an octagonal pavilion which, on the first floor, consisted of only a single room, the king's *salon*; on every side large windows looked out onto seven cages (the eighth side was reserved for the entrance), containing different species of animals. By Bentham's time, this menagerie had disappeared. But one finds in the programme of the Panopticon a similar concern with individualizing observation, with characterization and classification, with the analytical arrangement of space. The Panopticon is a royal menagerie; the animal is replaced by man, indvidual distribution by specific grouping and the king by the machinery of a furtive power. (Foucault 1995, 203)

The incorporating of power relations is, however, not limited to old-fashioned zoo architecture. Adorno (1974) claims that the replacement of bars by more invisible barriers such as water in zoo enclosures further emphasizes the denial of the liberation of the captives:

> Nor can any good come of Hagenbeck's layout, with trenches instead of cages, betraying the Ark by simulating the rescue that only Ararat can promise. They deny the animals' freedom only the more completely by keeping the boundaries invisible, the sight of which would inflame the longing for open spaces. /.../ The more purely nature is preserved and transplanted by civilization, the more implacably it is dominated. /.../ The fact, however, that animals really suffer more in cages than in the open range, that Hagenbeck does in fact represent a step forward in humanity, reflects on the inescapability of imprisonment. It is a consequence of history. The zoological gardens in their authentic form are products of nineteenth-century colonial imperialism. (Adorno 1974, 115-16)

Willis (1999) suggests that varied, innovative, and naturalized contemporary zoo designs (which have been described by Mullan and Marvin [1999] as the "architecture of guilt") may *increase* the visual domination of the animal. Different vantage points at different levels around the enclosure enhance the possibility of viewing animals from multiple angles. Willis parallels this form of the zoological gaze with vivisection, an absolute objectification of the animal, further emphasized by the plate-glass viewing wall commonly used at the zoo to exhibit aquatic animals. The glass slices the animal's aquatic world and makes it seem as if it has been bisected:

> An animal in the wild is integral with its surroundings, which it continuously engages through senses, instincts, and corporeal functions. To slice into an animal's environment, making its world a window for our gaze, enacts the surgery of invasion and domination. (Willis 1999, 681)

The purpose, as Willis sees it, is to create new forms of illusionary human-animal intimacy, having the contradictory effect of emphasizing our absolute separation from the animals. This separation makes the responses we get from the animals important to our zoo visit experience, that is, whether we can attract their attention and see them look back at us. However, our desire for the animal to return our look at the zoo often leads to disappointment since the animal is likely to ignore us (Rothfels 2002b).

In Berger's (1980) analysis, an animal's disinterest in the human spectator is because we "*are looking at something that has been rendered absolutely marginal*" (22, emphasis in original). According to Berger, the marginalization of animals is a consequence of them having been made completely dependent on their keepers, the artificiality of the spaces they inhabit in the zoo, and their isolation. Our ritual of looking at animals living in diaspora in the zoo (Hebert 2008) is important for our sense of self, but when we are denied acknowledgement by the animals, we may instead find *ourselves* isolated. The zoo then becomes a place of isolation for animals as well as for humans, quite contrary to its presumed function of acting as a site of encounter between the species. According to Rothfels (2002b), it is exactly the moment when the animal at the zoo actually *does* look back at us that has a destabilizing effect on the foundations of the zoo's existence as it forces us to reflect on the subjective experience of the animal.

School-zoo interfaces

The "exotic" and the "cartoonish"

Power relations enacted by the zoo extend beyond zookeepers' and zoo visitors' relations with the captive animals. Like other institutions, zoos may differ depending on the social and cultural context in which they are located, but Western zoos share a common legacy in the form of the old menageries.

The capturing of wild animals for zoo exhibits historically functioned as a material as well as a symbolic representation of the conquest of distant, exotic lands, and the zoos were thus an endorsement of colonial power through a visual display of imperial reach (Berger 1980; Davies 2000). Rothfels's (2002b) historical investigation into Hagenbeck's Animal Park in Germany describes a business not only in international hunting, trade, and exhibits of exotic species, but also in exhibits of indigenous people from all over the world, beginning in 1875 with "a family of Laplanders" (complete with a herd of reindeer and household belongings) brought to the park to complement the usual animal exhibits. This initiative was followed by exhibits of "Nubian," "Eskimo," and "Ceylonese" people.[1] The rationale for the people displays seems to have been similar to that for the display of exotic animals: to stimulate curiosity and fascination by means of a constructed encounter with "the other." Many of the menageries also exhibited humans with various sorts of deformations considered to deviate from the normative human appearance (Mullan & Marvin 1999).

The previous history of the zoo was not discussed in any class I visited. Although some of the learning materials used acknowledged the history of the menageries as ethically problematic, and that the animals kept there were often in miserable condition, the "people shows" such as those described by Rothfels (2002b) were not mentioned. The intertwining of human and animal otherness in the zoo was, however, referred to by Jeanette, a former animal caretaker student, during an informal interview:

> If all zoos disappeared, there is a risk that we would go back to looking at deformed people in tents. Sometimes we need to see things that we can't understand, but that are not threatening. Maybe we need fair amounts of this [experience]. Zoos fulfill the function of letting us see something that is different.

While the zoo has to a large extent reinvented itself and washed away its controversial legacy, one of the zoos visited in this study displayed an exoticizing logic in its zoogeographic organization by grouping its animals in the park according to their continent of origin (Asia, Africa, and South America), which was also marked by artefacts assumed to be significant for each continent and restaurants with exotically sounding names like "Bali," "Jambo," and "Pampas." The Asian area, for instance, had a Buddha statue and an entrance in the shape of a pagoda. Next to the entrance to the African area, a sign greeted us with the message "Welcome to Africa." Straw roofed huts accompanied the animal displays, ensuring that the geographical theme message did not go unnoticed. According to Mullan and Marvin (1999), this classical way of displaying animals not only attempts to convey a sense of the "exotic" by stressing the curiosity value, but also carries colonial connotations. Human and animal otherness is thus blended in the physical design of the park. Their description of Buenos Aires Zoo analyzes these features:

> /…/ animals on display were strange creatures from distant lands and that quality was emphasized by relating them to a series of images of the strange human societies which inhabited the same far-off places. Elements of human cultural styles became indicators of distance and difference and are used therefore as markers for the animals. (Mullan & Marvin 1999, 50)

Another approach is to give the interior of the animal enclosure an anthropomorphic and presumed humorous design. Mullan and Marvin (1999) show such an example at a Danish mini-zoo, where rabbits are housed in a "toy" village. One of the zoos visited during my field study had a similar display in their guinea pig enclosure. The guinea pig house was designed as a miniature replica of houses used for human activities. Such an exhibit not only anthropomorphizes the animals, it also trivializes and juvenilizes them; indeed, it makes them seem as cartoon-like as the Mickey Mouse figure decorating the entrance to the park. As Berger (1980) notes, zoo decors often resemble theatre props, making the animals appear like actors on a stage.

The zoological gaze is productive in the construction of the animals' otherness at the zoo. At one animal caretaker school, the first-year students were assigned to develop their visions of an entire animal park structure. Al-

though some of these student projects[2] emphasized the importance of providing sheltered areas for the animals where they can withdraw from the public,
there were also detailed ideas about how to provide unobstructed views of the
animals from as many angles as possible, such as underwater tunnels to observe
aquatic animals from below, cafes and conference rooms located with views
of animals from above, staircases, and binoculars. Some ideas reminded one
of the *Panopticon* structure, where the observed object cannot herself observe
(Foucault 1995):

> If a female [feline] animal is going to have babies, we take her into a
> special enclosure within the large inner enclosure, where she can be on
> her own with the babies. The size of that area is 40x40 meters and it has
> plants and a little lake, which is not filled with water when the babies are
> there due to the drowning risk. The enclosure is equipped with hidden
> video cameras so that both the staff and the visitors, on a TV at the
> info center, can see what is happening with the mother and the babies.
> (Quoted from student report, my translation)

The dolphin performance

Another dimension of animal otherness was embodied by the dolphin performance, compulsory in one school's zoo visit schedule and occupying a special
place and status. In the show, the dolphins are personalized and given names
and drawn into a sphere of intimacy and familiarity that conceptually distinguishes them from most other animals at the zoo:

> First, we are shown a promotion film about the sponsors of the zoo
> (among others, Coca Cola and GB Glace[3]) on a screen above the dolphin
> pool. The film goes on for quite a while. Thereafter a picture is projected
> onto the same screen showing free dolphins in the sea. Bengt, the teacher
> sitting beside me, turns to me and remarks that somehow they are not
> really the same *animals*, when you have seen them like that (in their
> natural habitat). I ask him what he thinks the difference is. He replies
> that it has to do with a feeling of freedom.

> During the show, the dolphins are made to perform different tasks while
> background music is playing. "Dolphins are cuddly animals and it is
> important for them, just as it is for us, with closeness and tenderness. So
> the best moments we have are down in the water," explains one trainer.
> She "dances" with the dolphins, kisses them, and rides across the pool
> standing upright on a dolphin's back. We are told that the basic premises
> for good cooperation between human and animal is respect, trust, and
> having fun together. After the show, some of the students approach their

teacher John and ask him to help them so that they can pat the dolphins, or get a job in the show.

To many of the students, the dolphin show's promise of human-animal symbio-sis seems to appear irresistible. A student I spoke to after the zoo visit viewed her chances of getting a job at the zoo—particularly in the dolphin show—as an unachievable dream. The opportunity for close encounters with normally "wild" animals (such as dolphins) appears to resonate deeply with the wishes and aspirations of the students. The emotive responses elicited by the per-formance build on an idea of shared sensory experiences and needs between humans and dolphins, manifested in the various acts during the show in an atmosphere of harmony and happiness.

The dolphin show experience can also be viewed in the light of Des-mond's (1995) observation of the orca whale performance at San Diego's Sea World. She notes that the hierarchy remains clear during the show, although somewhat hidden by rhetorical assertions of mutuality and equality. The show is controlled and choreographed by humans, and the animals are disciplined to deliver a rigorously planned performance through cues almost invisible to the spectator's eye. The story told by this performance is one with a veneer of interspecies intimacy and understanding, behind which the necessary relation of domination lies carefully concealed:

> The conditions of possibility for the show are that wild whales are captured, transported thousands of miles, confined, trained, and forced to work for a living. They make money /.../. To mask this reality, they are presented as willing partners, as part of our family, as equals from whom we have so much to learn, and their display is coded as art, as education, and as conservation. (Desmond 1995, 230)

Although these two zoo contexts certainly are different in terms of scale, in-vestment, and structure, their animal shows seem to exhibit similarities in meaning. The dolphin and whale performances both attempt to overcome animal otherness, but at the same time their existence paradoxically rests on the acknowledgment of this same otherness. Furthermore, despite their per-sonalized framework, the performing dolphins/whales are for educational purposes supposed to represent *all* animals of their species (much like the other animals at the zoo), but the dolphin show fails to fully achieve this. The teacher Bengt sees the dolphins as representing only their captive counterparts, whereas free dolphins are viewed as almost qualitatively different animal be-ings. The physical constraint of confinement is forced not only onto the animals themselves, but also onto how they are perceived. For many of the students, however, the coercive relations in the dolphin performance are glossed over by its emotional impact.

Legitimation strategies and moments of resistance

A threefold basis of justification for keeping animals in captivity could be traced in the zoo rhetoric and was also reproduced by the schools: species preservation, research and education, and recreation. According to Hanson (2002), a rationale behind these goals is to imply that zoos have something to offer for everyone, which helps account for their lasting popularity. At one animal caretaker program, this narrative of preservation, research, education, and recreation was conveyed to all new students from their first introduction day as *the* ethical rationale for keeping animals in captivity, in the school as well as at the zoo. The rationale was presented as self-evident and non-negotiable. The learning material used enforced the message, such as the following example from the other animal caretaker school:

> The animals keep their fingers crossed. Who will help the animals when things start to go bad? Yes, the zoos of the world! Endangered animals worth protecting have real friends in the zoos of today. Some of the animals would not exist on the earth at all if zoos had not existed. (*Bevare oss väl!*, 172, my translation)

Also zoos themselves emphasized their active involvement in species preservation projects. My interviews with students, however, did reveal some ethical concerns. Carina, an animal caretaker student in her third year, expressed the following view:

> Sure, I think it is *terrible* to keep animals in captivity. It is, it is not fun at all, I think. But for the purposes of research, being able to care for the animals outside and preserve them, it is important to learn about the animals and be able to, well, be able to teach as well. In that case it is good to have animals as we have them here at the school as well. So, I really don't think that it is *right* to have animals like that. But for educational purposes and research and to be able to care for the animals in nature, it is important, I think.

Carina's ambivalence toward keeping animals in captivity seems to emanate from an ethical conflict of interest between the captive individuals and the animals "in nature," who in the end are those who presumably will benefit. In a social science class on animal ethics with a group of second-year students from Carina's school, the teacher Anna raised the same issue:

> Now, Anna wants to bring up a new question for discussion: Do they [the students] think that it is OK to keep reptiles and other such animals in

> a cage, whose natural environment is never possible to fully reconstruct, like they have at the school? One student replies with a defense of her school: We have them [the animals] for a purpose, she says, just as the zoos do. Our purpose is education. Anna: You will educate yourselves in order to make things better for other animals, therefore it is OK that they [the animals kept at school] suffer for a while? Anna gets the reply that they [the animals] are bred in a terrarium, and that they wouldn't survive outside. /.../ The next comment from the student group is: We would never keep animals ourselves as many other people do, because we learn how those animals ought to be kept.

When encouraged to reflect on an ethically problematic practice, the students defend not only their own roles, but their school's role as well, seeing both parties as a medium through which to achieve a better life for animals in their natural habitat. The fact that most of the captive animal individuals fulfill a solely instrumental role in this process and are denied a life in freedom gives rise to ethical concerns. These concerns are alleviated by the argument that the means justifies the end, and in this sense the critical thinking taking place in the classroom was typically accommodated within the existing zoo paradigm. However, during a lesson about endangered species conservation at the other animal caretaker school, the teacher Bengt brings a fundamental argument for the zoo enterprise into question:

> "We use these lifetime prisoners [the animals at zoos] for research, when we have captured them," says Bengt, and asks his students: "Is it right, do you think, to capture (and do research on) wild animals? How many baby dolphins have died in the pools of [name of zoo]? /.../ How many monkeys have died during transportation?" Bengt says that sometimes the idea of conservation threatens wild species. His invitation to his students to critically reflect on the zoo paradigm did not, however, give rise to any classroom discussion, and the focus shifted quickly to another issue.

The visits to zoos gave rise to varied reactions among the students. Their joy at seeing the animals was mixed with feelings of pity for at least some of them, such as the polar bear and the gorilla. When I asked the first-year student Johanna what she thought about one of the zoos visited, she described her experience as follows:

> It was boring; the animals "just stand there." The enclosures were boring. The animals had nowhere to hide.

Johanna's disappointment about the animals' lethargy resonates well with Berger's (1980) analysis, summarized in the question "Why are these animals

less than I believed?" (21). One of the zoos triggered particularly strong reactions among the students. When strolling through the park, I heard numerous
critical remarks and nauseated exclamations concerning the poor conditions
for the animals kept there. In the reptile house, I meet Marianne, a student
in her first year. She is very upset, trying to find out whether it is possible for
anybody to actually open one of the glass cages, and after a little while she
manages to do it. When John, her teacher, shows up, she explodes in an angry
monologue about how easy it would be to take animals out of the zoo. John
tries to calm her down, saying that there is a purpose with the visit. (The purpose, as it was explained to me, was to expose the students to a "bad" zoo to
enhance their critical thinking.) I walk with Marianne back to our bus. She
is still very upset and says to me that she hates this park:

> Would they put their children in that chimpanzee cage, she asks angrily.
> I reply that they would probably not. But they put chimpanzees there,
> "our closest relative!!" she exclaims. Marianne tells me that many of her
> classmates had chosen to go to the amusement park instead (an integrated
> part of this zoo), as they couldn't stand seeing the conditions in which
> the animals were kept.

Codes and norms of watching wildlife

Zoos were not the only sites where animals were observed as part of the curriculum. There were also school excursions to nature reserves, and, in additi-
ton, numerous wildlife films shown to the students in their classrooms. Both
activities are ways of seeing with a common denominator: The idea that we are
entering into the animals' *own* world (cf. Desmond 1999). Watching wildlife—
whatever the medium—is therefore an activity that can be expected to differ
from a zoo or museum visit experience. Acampora (2005) has emphasized
these contrasts by pointing out that observation *in situ* allows the animals to
choose whether to engage in or break off any encounter with human visitors.
This animal agency offers a perceived authenticity that also carries a connota-
tion of "appropriateness": A possibility to catch a glimpse of animals "as they
should be seen"—that is, undisturbed by human society (cf. Baker 2001).

My field study offered plenty of opportunities to observe learning situations centered around activities involving watching wildlife in nature and on
film, since the animal caretaker programs in Sweden to a large extent lack ad-
equate textbooks that relate to their subject areas such as zoo management and
ethology. This situation imposes extra responsibility on the teachers to produce
their own collection of materials such as readers, field study assignments, and

also films. One teacher showed me a media archive register he had created, comprising over two hundred pages of recorded wildlife films and press clippings stored over a period of six to seven years. The reason for creating such a register, he told me, was that there are no textbooks on zoos.

The students received guidance in various ways regarding what to pay attention to in situations involving watching wildlife. When watching wildlife films, typically, the voice-over was the primary guide, complemented by the teacher who could interrupt the film narrative by turning the video off for a few moments to add comments or write key words on the whiteboard. On excursions, the voice-over was replaced by comments by school staff or by written materials. In either case, students were asked to focus on roughly three different dimensions of the animals: Their *physical bodies* and *behaviors*, the *number* of species and individuals, and *aesthetic* or *"spiritual"* qualities of the wildlife encounter.

Animal behavior

One set of characteristics that students were expected to pay attention to included the physical appearance, behavior, and adaptability in animals. Feeding behavior, in particular predator-prey interactions, are frequently focused on in many wildlife films and, according to Bousé (2000), probably disproportionately in relation to the real daily routines of many predator and prey animals. Bousé attributes this tendency to the demands on wildlife films for drama and climax:

> We may be told on the voice track that of a certain predator's attempts to catch prey only one in ten ends in a kill, but we certainly do not see nine failures for every one success. (Bousé 2000, 182)

For Burt (2001), animal deaths on film are a particularly charged form of animal representation that reflects not only a "voyeuristic" streak, but also a tension between the humane and the cruel, between education and entertainment. This tension was explicitly expressed in a film entitled *When Dogs Smile and Chimpanzees Cry*, brought to an ethology class by a second-year student:

> The film displays the headline "Mother and child." "The most characteristic quality of the mammals is to give care," says the voice-over as the film shows sea lion babies. When a sea lion baby is eaten by a killer whale, the voice-over expresses compassion. He says that he does not want to see this happening, even if it is a fantastic display of predator behavior. We are shown the reactions of the sea lion mother as she realizes that her baby is gone. "Heartbreaking," comments the voice-over.

The focus on how bodies look, what they do, and where they do it (Desmond 1999) as a guideline for watching wildlife can also be understood as observing *the right animal in the right place*. During a birdwatching excursion we passed by a cow enclosure. A few students stopped by the enclosure (instead of gazing out over the sea to observe the birds on the other side):

> A few students notice the flies gathering on the back on one of the cows and express feelings of pity. The teacher John passes by and comments on the fact that his students are watching cows instead of birds. Jokingly, he asks one of the girls, who is holding a bird guidebook in her hands, if she can find any cows in the book. Some students continue their walk, but a few stay by the cows for a while and observe them. They remark silently that one cow has an infection in her eye.

Much like ecotourism, certain animal species are coded as proper gazing targets and others as not (even though both may exist in the same habitat). As Desmond (1999) notes, the point of these activities is to access uniqueness, to come close to animals that are not normally visible in our daily lives: "Watching cockroaches in the kitchen or rabbits in the backyard doesn't count as ecotourism" (169). This norm may be violated by students as a protest against the perceived dullness of the birdwatching experience, or as a way of changing its meaning by adding fun to it:

> The first-year student Johanna tells me that she finds the birdwatching exercise uninteresting as you can't really see anything – just a tiny dot that is flying. /.../ She tells me about a previous birdwatching occasion, when they had zoomed in on cows with their binoculars instead of birds.

> We continue our walk through the reeds. Where the path turns and the forest begins, we stop to wait for the rest of the group. Daniel and Per stand behind me. Daniel asks Per what we all are looking at as we stand facing the sea. "The sheep over there," Per replies jokingly.

Domestic animals function here as a comical antithesis to the "real" targets of wild birds and do not count as "proper" targets. To be ascribed value in this context, the animal has to be a bird and it has to be *wild* (Donnelly 1994). This characteristic was expressed as "spontaneously emerging" in the list of bird species the students received as a guide for their birdwatching (*Miniförteckning över Sveriges fåglar* 2004).

Counting

Another dimension the students were encouraged to focus on concerned the *quantity* of animals, in terms of both number of individuals and species, and this was of particular importance to the birdwatching exercise. During a visit to a bird observatory, we learned from our guide that a "good" year (and a "good" day) at the research station is when many birds are caught, since keeping statistics on bird populations and their variations is a main task of the research work at the observatory. Similarly, in the written information provided to the students by their teachers in preparation for the excursion, it was stated that "On a 'good' day [in April] 100,000 birds [eiders] can pass by!" (*Fåglar* 2004).

Birdwatching is thus primarily about (symbolic) *collecting*, preferably of rarities (Donnelly 1994; Sheard 1999). The birdwatching excursion was a ritualized activity that strongly adhered to these formal elements (albeit in a leisurely atmosphere):

> We left our hostel very early in the morning. A list has been distributed among the students, *Miniförteckning över Sveriges fåglar* ("Mini list of Sweden's birds"), with all wild domestic bird species listed. The idea is that the students, divided into small groups, will try to see as many species as possible, and tick them off on the list. The group finding the largest number of species will be rewarded with a prize. The teacher Bengt tells us what is considered as cheating and the students have been equipped with binoculars and bird guidebooks. The teachers carry additional equipment. Bengt instructs us how we can distinguish between bird species by the sound of their singing.

To one student, Sanna, the birdwatching exercise ends in an unexpected way. On the bus home, all the groups are asked to report about how many bird species they have been able to tick off on the list. The winning students, who have seen far more than fifty species, are rewarded with a bag of candies as the first prize. Sanna, who is sitting beside me on the bus, belongs to the group that came second. Her group has also found more than fifty species:

> Suddenly Sanna finds a tiny green caterpillar on her hand. The teacher Bengt sees it too, and says with faked seriousness that Sanna must return to the excursion site and leave it there, since the caterpillar won't like a new environment. Sanna, however, apparently does not perceive this as a joke. After a few minutes of thinking, she takes her bird list on which she has ticked off the fifty plus species and starts tearing it apart. She carefully constructs a small paper box out of the list. I ask her if I can help her by holding the caterpillar while she is folding the box. She nods and places the caterpillar in my hands. When she is finished she holds up the box and I place the caterpillar in it. Then she finishes her construction by folding the last paper flap over it as a cover, and attaches the box to the seat pocket in front of her for safe transportation of the caterpillar back home.

Sanna creatively changes the function and meaning of her bird list by putting it to *concrete* use. As her successful symbolic collection of birds is transformed into a temporary housing for the caterpillar, the focus is also shifted from the quantifiable and "countable" aspects that structured the birdwatching exercise, to the intrinsic value and welfare of an individual creature.

Aesthetics and emotions

Some wildlife watching situations encouraged a gaze that could be described as *spiritual*. According to Pierson (2005), some nature films represent nature "as a great eternal moral and spiritual entity," invoking the idea of "the Great Chain of Being" of which all creatures are part (709). A part of this image is what Bousé (2000) defines as the tendency to depict "visual splendor" in wildlife; magnificent scenery that suggests a still-unspoiled, primeval wilderness, and a sense of timelessness where the presence of humans is concealed (14-15).

In ecotourism settings, Desmond (1999) has formulated the spiritual dimension in religious terms as special pilgrimages to sacred and utopian sites of purity, communicated through both the ritualized procedures for access and behavior at the site and in the hushed voices and the sense of awe evoked by the scene. Desmond's description is not very far from the following evening visit to a seal colony—a voluntary activity that a lot of students nevertheless chose to join:

> The bus trip to the site takes a long time. The bus has to stop at the beginning of the path leading to the sea, as it may not be able to turn around further ahead. The teacher Bengt says that he doesn't know whether there will be any seals there at all, but if we want to see any, we must be very quiet. It is quite a long walk, thirty to forty minutes.

> When we reach the shore, the sun is setting. A huge full moon shines behind us. Soon we discover a couple of seals some distance out in the water. The students are silent, observe the seals through their binoculars and appear to be moved by the experience. John turns to me and remarks that this is a different thing compared to seeing them [the seals] at a zoo, a more powerful sight somehow. "They are as curious as we are," he says. Madeleine, a student standing next to me, lends me her binoculars so that I can see the seals better. Kristina who is standing beside us says that it is really an experience to see them free.

> It is getting dark and we start walking back to our bus. On the way I speak with Sanna. I say to her that when you are used to seeing seals as zoo animals, seeing them free becomes something special. Sanna agrees and says it makes you think about the situation of the seals in the zoo.

The seal watching experience is framed as one of "minimal constructedness" that is ascribed value as a "truer" real (Desmond 1999, 190) on the basis of contrasting it to the zoo context. Appreciation of the aesthetics and tranquility of both the animals and the entire nature scene visited was not only an added dimension of the wildlife watching experience, but occasionally also a response explicitly or implicitly *expected* of the students. This was also suggested in the written learning material compiled by the teachers prior to the birdwatching excursion, which stated that "Looking at birds is first and foremost amusing, but it is also easy to be impressed and amazed!" (*Fåglar* 2004). Not all the students, however, conformed to the "prescribed" gaze of awe:

> On our walk through the forest Johanna criticizes the birdwatching exercise to Kerstin, one of the school staff members. Johanna's voice sounds as if she is bored. She complains that she finds the activity pointless. Kerstin replies that the birdwatching experience is about atmospheres and moods that nobody can give Johanna, but which she must discover herself.

Receptivity to the "spiritual" dimension seems to be, if not an explicit part of the learning objectives, at least a characteristic desirable to instill in the students, who also receive guidance from the school implying that it is more or less expected behavior.

Animal and human society in wildlife films: Comparisons and analogies

Although wildlife films are about nature, they are cultural products with values that tend to permeate the film scenery and narrative and affect the way they are viewed (Mitman 1999; Bousé 2000; Pierson 2005). According to Bousé (2000), wildlife films have a great potential for naturalizing ideological values. They are often produced in a manner that lets us "find" in nature, for instance, "virtues" of personal responsibility such as devotion to the nuclear family, diligence, courage, commitment, and self-sacrifice. The following example is a sequence from the film entitled *When Dogs Smile and Chimpanzees Cry*[4] shown in an ethology class:

> The voice-over mentions "loyalty" and "compassion," previously believed to be found only in humans. One example is a mongoose. The film shows a mongoose that has confronted a jackal and gets weaker and weaker from her injuries. She won't survive on her own in the desert. The flock slows down to give the injured member a chance to keep up, but eventually she gets so weak that she collapses. The entire mongoose family returns to her, and won't leave her. She didn't die alone. The film then asks the

question: "What is the difference?" What is it that distinguishes human beings from all other living creatures?

When the teacher (who has been absent during the film) comes back, she asks her class to give a summary of what the film was about. The words "sorrow" and "soul" are mentioned. One student remarks that the animals have a soul, not only learned behavior.

The "hero" theme was also discernible. In the film *Ghosts of the Great Salt Lakes*, showing hyena research, the main research subject is given the name "Bom" (which, according to the film, is a common name among "bushmen"). At the end of the film, when another hyena is found dead (run over by a car), Bom is found uninjured, and the researcher, Glynn, can reunite with him. The voice-over concludes: "Bom and Glynn have reunited /.../ Glynn, like Bom, is a wanderer at heart. Two soulmates /.../." The story line here resembles the traditional genre of Western films that "usually center on strong, heroic leading characters who outlive the weaklings that surround them" (Bousé 2000, 162-63).

A few films explicitly stated that it is possible to ascribe human emotions to animals, and when we study them, another picture of animals' emotions takes shape. This was the message of the film *When Dogs Smile and Chimpanzees Cry*. However, it also conveyed a moral lesson on what constitutes a "good mother":

> The voice-over talks about elephants: "It is known that elephants are good mothers." A film team followed a flock of elephants with a newborn baby with a leg deformation making it difficult for it to stand up. The students exclaim "No!" as they watch the baby elephant's problems. We are shown how the mother tries to help her baby to stand up. "Oh, how terrible!" says one student. When the flock moves on and the baby is unable to keep up, it starts making sounds. One of the elephants in the flock runs back to the baby. Then two of the elephants walk slowly to wait for it. The voice-over says that the mother is old and experienced, and knows what she must do for her baby. She gives it time to practise standing up.

Responsible parenting was also the issue in the following sequence from the film *The Zebra—The Striped Horse* shown in a zoo management class:

> The film shows a zebra foal and plays soft background music. The voice-over says, "The family flock wanders in ranking order. /.../ Also the males must look after the little foals but that is not always an easy task, since the foals are both lively and mischievous." The film shows a foal that has run astray. When the foal makes a noise, a male zebra finds it

and brings it back to the flock. "The mother is angry at the foal that ran away," says the voice-over.

Wildlife films not only project human (typically Western) social and cultural patterns and moral categories on nature, but also allow us to see our own familiar structures and values enacted among wildlife in ways that reconfirm them as *natural*, as universal biological "truths" rather than as social constructs (Bousé 2000). Ganetz (2004) refers to this double process as a "cultural boomerang" (209). Also this message was explicitly expressed when watching some films, such as *How do they know?*:

> The teacher Robert turns the video on. The voice-over introduces the film with the statement "By studying the behavior of other animals, we can also learn more about ourselves." Robert focuses on kangaroos. He speaks about *survival of the fittest* and *the winner takes it all* (referring to the famous ABBA pop song) among newborn kangaroo babies. One student asks if the baby is aware of what it is doing. Robert replies that "it absolutely does not know about anything whatsoever."
>
> He turns the video on again. The film now speaks about the phenomenon of imprinting. Robert writes on the whiteboard:
>
> "2) *Wildebeest* calf is *imprinted* at birth"
>
> Robert says that researchers have attached wildebeest hides to poles in order to see if wildebeest babies will run to the poles. "This has been done to monkey babies too, rather *horrible* experiments," Robert remarks. He makes an analogy to what happens to humans who are not allowed to grow up in a natural environment: They develop aggressiveness, lack of empathy. He compares with gang formations among humans that build on solidarity through exclusion.

When biological "models" are used to explain aspects of human society and political and sociological factors are downplayed or ignored, as in the above extrapolation of wildebeest and monkey deprivation to humans, complex and problematic human social conditions may appear simplistic and even predetermined. Together with the "survival of the fittest" and "the winner takes it all" image of the natural world as a game between winners and losers, the approach accords with what Bousé (2000) calls "Darwinian projections": an implication that our own social organization and economic theories are natural laws of society.

Critical perspectives on wildlife films

Bousé (2000) applies a critique of wildlife films in an analogy with the critique of Hollywood-style filmmaking that was developed by some film theorists in the British journal *Screen* in the 1970s. Bousé argues for the wider applicability of this critique on the grounds that wildlife films largely derive their formal structure from the Hollywood conventions of film production, although they explicitly claim to represent "the real." The critique focused both on the ontology of visual images in realist cinema (i.e., the notion that film simply is an expression of reality) as well as on its ideological tendency to simplify the complexities of reality. The critics argued that a kind of false consciousness is systematically promoted when motion pictures represent reality through a series of multileveled fictions or narratives:

> According to this perspective, events that are contingent appear inevitable; situations that are contrived appear natural; actions and values that derive from culture appear to derive from nature; society's rules thus appear as "natural laws". (Bousé 2000, 17)

This way of producing film narratives makes the values of the dominant culture and its hierarchies appear "natural," legitimized, and immutable to change (Bousé 2000). As an example, Chris (2006) mentions the heteronormativity[5] that has largely structured the wildlife film genre as in their preoccupation with births and parenting, which were also alluded to in films shown at my field schools (cf. Ganetz 2004). The ideological overtones may be further illustrated by the representation of "otherized" humans in wildlife films. In the early twentieth century wildlife film era, many films had the form of exploration trips that documented white expeditions in colonized territories. Besides establishing wildlife filmmaking as a largely masculine project and as a manifestation of imperialist rights to global natural resources, these films also articulated racial ideologies for popular consumption (Chris 2006). Ganetz (2004) remarks that historically, white people have not appeared in wildlife films except as masters, experts, or presenters of nature, whereas native peoples have usually appeared in the role of bearers or as part of the landscape. Like the tradition of museums and zoos that juxtaposes indigenous peoples with wildlife and in this way reproduces a conception of their position as "closer to nature," the presence of people of color in wildlife films may still serve a similar purpose and reinforce conventional stereotypes:

> The teacher Robert turns the film on. He writes the film title, "*How Do They Know* (cont.)," on the whiteboard. One sequence is about the nesting behavior of a certain finch species. "Here you will see something really,

really funny," comments Robert. The female finch tests the strength of the nest built by the male. When the nest collapses, Robert and the students laugh. He comments that it must be tough to build a nest without any tools, just a beak: "It is skillful anyway to be able to do something like this with only a beak," he says, and adds that he has tried it himself. Thereafter, the film shows people weaving grass baskets. Robert describes how the people, who are from Namibia, proceed when they work. One student asks, "What the hell do they think [when white filmmakers come to them]?" Robert then refers to "cultural clashes" and remarks that these may become even more devastating in the future.

In this example, in the film, the native people and the wildlife in the area are both sorted under the category of exotic "others." In contrast to the Western researchers in the film entitled *Ghosts of the Great Salt Lakes*, the native people are observed when performing manual labor and depicted without any heroic, intellectual, or authoritative aura (cf. Jernudd 2000).

In none of these classroom situations involving watching wildlife films were the meanings, values, or production methods of the films discussed.[6] In the classroom, the messages of the films were normally treated as mirrors of "reality," but this does not necessarily mean that students internalize what Bousé (2000) refers to as "false consciousness" (17). Jeanette, a former student, told me about how her choice of profession as an animal caretaker has influenced her zoological gaze, also in her leisure time:

You get to see animals in another way after some time. You don't want to watch nature films anymore, unless there is something that you really have a special interest in, since you switch on your professional gaze all the time. This also applies to animals you meet in your leisure time: you immediately look at what their fur looks like, what breed and sex they are, and so on. /.../ I get annoyed when animals in nature films are given [personal] names, or when the filmmakers add smacking sounds when the animals eat. Moreover, in nature films they choose which animals are "good" and which are "bad": The audience may never see when a group of dolphins takes a female away from her flock to rape her for several days before bringing her back to her flock again.

Conclusions

In both zoo visits and wildlife watching activities we find reflections of different notions of human-animal relations intertwined with ideas of similarities and dissimilarities between humans and animals. As school activities, observation of animals took place in different settings and with different degrees of formalization, but was in general structured by explicit or implicit expectations regarding the students as to *what* to look for, *how* to look, and how to *respond* to their observations.

There seems to be more to observing animals than just formal learning of basic ethological facts and consolidation of a shared professional and scientific framework. Firstly, implicit messages about both animal and human society are present at zoos as well as in wildlife films, messages that enable certain human-animal relations and disable others. In zoos, the physical design of the setting is at the same time an effect of, and helps producing, arrangements of visually oriented power relations manifested by humans over animals. Especially when these arrangements carry colonial overtones, certain human as well as animal positions are created and intimately tied to each other.

Secondly, teaching about animal behavior by making references to human behavior is often a pedagogically motivated approach, but may also imply a hidden curriculum manifested as a lesson in character education with several layers of values and meanings. In wildlife films, this hidden curriculum may on the one hand be seen as an anthropomorphic imposition onto the animal world of values and structures recognizable from above all contemporary Western society. On the other hand, a reversal projection seems to be taking place when biologically determined models of explanations evoked in wildlife films are applied to human society. As Bousé (2000) has suggested, the projection process thus operates in two parallel directions and in this manner both reinforces and universalizes its messages.

Notes

1. "People shows" still occur in zoos. In June 2005, an entire African village with people, animals, and handicrafts was exhibited at a zoo in Germany, and similar events took place in zoos in London, Bedfordshire, and Detroit (Raji 2005). In 2006, a debate arose about a Masai show in a Swedish zoo. According to the zoo, the Masai performers were hired to market safari trips to Kenya (*Svenska Dagbladet* August 2, 2006).

2. I read seven student reports on this subject.

3. GB Glace is an ice cream-producing company.

4. This film was not really a wildlife film, although it contained sequences of filmed wildlife.

5. Chris (2006) notes that when homosexuality is represented in wildlife films, it is usually free from the associations between animal and human behavior that often accompany heterosexual representations as well as other aspects of animal life in the genre.

6. In animal protection classes, where the objectives were not primarily to learn basic facts about the animal species dealt with, the pedagogical approach was somewhat more critical and as far as wildlife or other animal related films were used as learning materials in these classes, a critical analysis of their messages was often encouraged.

Chapter 5

"The fantastic world of the Lion King." Animals and commodification processes

Introduction

As part of most human-animal relations, animals are commodified in various ways. Emel and Wolch (1998) have identified the "animal economy" as comprising globalized animal agribusiness; ecological cleansing in the intensification of land-use; hunting and fishing; the capturing, trading and breeding of wild animals for circuses, laboratories, pets, trophies, sport, and other purposes; and biotechnology. Many of these practices are the focus of heavy investments from private and public actors:

> Over the past two decades, the animal economy has become simultaneously both more intensive and more extensive. More profits are squeezed out of each animal life, more quickly, while the reach of animal-based industries has grown to include most of the developing world. (Emel & Wolch 1998, 2)

The ways by which education systems take part in the global web of the animal economy are reflected in everyday school activities, which—as we shall see—sometimes get intertwined with corporate branding and identity strategies of big-name companies. Most wildlife films, for instance, are industrialized commodities that must be adapted to the economic and institutional agendas of the producing companies and be sold for profit on a competitive global media market. Camera images are manipulated, intensified, dramatized, and fictionalized to reflect certain views, typically those of the countries that produce and export the majority of the films or the countries with the largest audiences (Bousé 2000). The presence of economic interests also appears in zoo management and hunter education, as well as in processes of meat and dairy-centered food socialization in which the school plays a significant role. These aspects are addressed in the present chapter.

Animal trade and breeding in zoos

Zoos perform a multifaceted commodification process in respect of the zoo's history as well as its present forms. Hanson (2002) notes that wealth-accumulating civilizations have long been interested in collecting exotic animals, and the animal trade that zoos (as well as circuses, the pet trade, and laboratories) have relied on was a form of colonial commerce dependent on the structures set up by European powers in Africa and Asia. The collection of animals displayed at zoos in the late nineteenth century was thus shaped less by their representativity across the taxonomic order, but by what was available for sale on the market (Hanson 2002). Zoos sought to enhance their status by comparing their animal collections with scientific and cultural institutions such as museums[1] and distinguish themselves from circuses, but Hanson (2002) notes that there were in fact several overlaps between zoos and circuses since they often exchanged both animals and personnel and relied on the same animal dealers.

Contemporary zoos have made efforts to shake off their controversial legacy and create a new basis of justification for their existence. For this purpose, a Noah's Ark metaphor of biodiversity conservation is useful since it evokes an image of a sanctuary where different animal species live peacefully side by side, protected from the brutal realities they face in nature (Rothfels 2002a). The Noah's Ark metaphor has also suited the vision of the zoo planners, since a breeding pair of every species would spare the zoo the future expense of buying animals (Hanson 2002). The Ark metaphor in itself, however, is a too superficial way of understanding the contemporary zoo. In Anderson's (1998) analysis, zoos can be seen as a form of "hybrid spaces," located at the culture-nature interface—an arena in which humans have defined and struggled with their complex relationship to animals and nature. It is a place for the discursive construction of animal otherness and human identity, as well as for the situated material production of human-animal relations. Malamud (1998) offers a Marxist analysis of the latter:

> The representations of animals in zoos and zoo stories are indebted to the machinations of capitalism and the agenda of capitalist hegemony.

> The energy—physical, financial, cultural—that goes into the acquisition
> of captive animals and the proliferation of zoos as institutions reflects
> the 'magnitude' that Greenblatt (following Marx) sees as an essential
> constituent, or force, of modern capitalist culture. (Malamud 1998, 11)

Malamud sees zoos as embodying an accumulation of "capital" in the local culture, which is illustrated, for example, when a local zoo is described as an investment in the region where it is located. Contrary to the story of the zoo as a raiser of awareness of endangered species, the demands that the zoo be profitable contradict its self-declared aims: The animals are resituated "in a place that could hardly be further from nature—surrounded by parking lots, gift shops, and hot-dog stands" (Malamud 2003, B9). Despite this, zoos sell the idea of a vanishing "wilderness" as one of the last bastions of idealized authenticity—regardless of whether the animals exhibited have ever seen wilderness or not (Desmond 1995).

After World War II, zoos could no longer rely on the wild animal trade as suppliers of their collections and turned to captive breeding. Breeding ensures continuous availability of animals to display as well as public sympathy when zoos can show that they are part of the effort to save species rather than contributing to their extinction. In addition, zoo births are taken as evidence that the zoo gives the animals good care and also draw crowds to the zoo (Hanson 2002).[2] Therefore, at a zoo, not only animal behavior, but also their births and deaths are processes under strict human control. This message was conveyed to the students in a number of ways during my field study. For instance, during the showing of a zoo film from the United States, the reproduction problems of giant pandas were in focus.[3] The artificial insemination of these animals was explained with reference to the same procedure cows are exposed to in the agriculture industry and celebrated as an indication of progress in zoological research. The rationale behind the modern version of the Ark is not, however, simply to accommodate "two of every kind being ushered safely into a better future world" (Rothfels 2002a, 217). Animal reproduction is also a planned procedure calculated to fit into the zoo's marketing strategies:

> The teacher speaks about the time of the year when the zoo opens its
> gates to the public—which corresponds to the school's open house event
> the students arrange in their third year. "It is important to see to it that
> you have [animal] babies when the zoo opens," he remarks, and says that
> there is nothing [else] that attracts so much. The timing is important:
> "When should I put the animals together *in order* for their babies to be
> born *by* April 1?"

Zoos and corporate branding

There are other manifestations of animal commodification at zoos than the calculated reproduction of the captive animal collection. Another example emphasized in zoo management education was the integration of corporate identities into the zoo's profile. At one animal caretaker school, the animal facilities were designed with inspiration from a number of famous zoos world-wide to present an experience closely reminiscent of that of a "real" zoo. From an interview with one of the teachers, I understood that the Disney theme park Animal Kingdom in Florida had been an important source of influence for the school. Staff members had made study visits to the park, and one of them had even been employed there, and Animal Kingdom was sometimes referred to during lessons as a good example of various practical arrangements at a zoo. Also, when students were trained to guide visitors around, "infotainment" was a regularly occurring keyword, defined by the teacher as "knowledge and show business together."

In these zoo management classes, the importance of commercial think-ing was frequently pointed out to the students. Commodification of the ex-hibited animals' symbolic value by selling "zouvenirs" and arranging special events, performances, adventures, and working with sponsors and the enter-tainment industry were promoted as necessary ways of raising funds to run the zoo, consequently saving more animal species. But these arguments were frequently presented to the students in an ambivalent manner:

> The teacher Karin says [to her class] that some people think it is terrible with lotteries and merry-go-rounds, that they don't belong with animals. She says that it is a bit ambiguous, but that zoos have to attract people, and that a result may be that those who then go there [to the zoo] learn something they never could have imagined prior to [their visit].

During my fieldwork, first-year students were assigned to develop their visions of an entire animal park structure as a school project. Many of the students' fictitious zoos, as described in their written reports, reproduced a commercial-ized, capitalist logic, more or less commodifying the animals involved and the promise of intimate encounters with them.[4] Hotels, conference sites, amuse-ment parks, playgrounds, elephant rides, dolphin and seal shows, "zoovenir" shops, and various other activities designed to maximize the entertainment and economic exchange value of the animals were frequent elements in the student reports. One report was given a title inspired by the Disney movie *The Lion King*, with characters from the movie re-created in various forms throughout the park. The animal species were selected to fit in with the Disney theme, and some individuals were named after the movie characters. Thus, the animals are not only exposed as being representative of their species, but are also reconstructed as movie stars and incorporated in the brand of a multinational corporation. The front page of the report showed a picture from the movie, together with the following text:

> Welcome to the fantastic world of the Lion King, where you can see, among other things, lions, baboons, warthogs, slender-tailed meerkats, elephants and many other animals from the famous movie "The Lion King"! (Quoted from student report, my translation)

The schools I visited also went on study visits to various zoos as part of the regular curriculum. The students were given assignments to solve in the parks, such as classifying the animal species in the zoo, studying how the park is designed and managed, looking for stereotypical behaviors in the animals, and finding out how many conservation projects the park is participating in. At one school (whose zoo visit was one in a series of three; called "the golden zoo triangle" by one of the teachers), the students were informed that the zoo they were going to visit is an extremely good example of a zoo, whereas at the other school, the students were not given any prior information regarding the quality of the zoos. At all three zoos we visited, the presence of commercial interests made itself felt before any animals were encountered. At two of the zoos, the logotypes of sponsoring companies, such as GB Glace (an ice cream producer) and McDonald's confronted the visitor inside the zoo entrance. The sponsors were also allocated space on the information signs next to the animal enclosures and/or in the free information leaflets available in the parks. At the third zoo, a gigantic, artificial clown figure was sitting on top of the entrance building with a Mickey Mouse statue in one hand and an elephant statue in the other. On the lawn outside the entrance, there was a big Santa Claus statue. The three zoos were also equipped with conference centers, swimming pools, performance stages, amusement parks, and/or playing areas with designs inspired by well-known cartoon figures and names such as "Phantom Land" (*Fantomenland*).

After one zoo visit, the students were instructed how to design information signs at a zoo. As a good example, the teacher Robert mentioned a Disney theme park where the signs have been decorated with Disney characters together with children's nursery rhymes. Robert stresses that this approach is very stimulating and that information must be adjusted to the different age levels of the visitors. Furthermore, the zoo's sponsors must be visible on the signs:

But it must not look like this, he says (Robert draws a big sign on the whiteboard entirely covered by McDonald's logotype):

The name or logotype of the sponsor must not be too dominating. The purpose is not to have the visitors suddenly leave the park when they want to go and have a hamburger. A better way to do it is to write a line at the bottom of the sign, for instance, "Thank you, McDonald's, for your kindness /.../ You have been able to save this animal species." The way to do it is to incorporate the sponsor's name in a sentence. Robert writes on the whiteboard: "Sponsor's name included, please!!" He gives an example of a park that has all the sponsor names gathered together on a sign at the zoo entrance, but says that this doesn't work: people are not interested in stopping and reading it. /.../

According to Beardsworth and Bryman (2001), the simultaneous presence of Disney and McDonald's in a zoo context is not a coincidence. One of the sponsors of the Disney theme park Animal Kingdom is McDonald's. Disney's and McDonald's joint rationale for doing business is thus projected onto the zoo concept. A paradoxical effect is that the zoo, claiming to save and preserve animals, closely cooperates with an enterprise (McDonald's) whose business idea relies on the mass exploitation of them.

Animal agribusiness in school

Schools mediate not only knowledge, "facts," and ways of thinking, but also values, norms, and habits. Food socialization is one example. As part of the socialization into meat and dairy consumption, commodification of animals in the agriculture industry was reproduced in some school textbooks. In a chapter on genetics in a natural science textbook, the cattle breed *Belgian Blue* is called "a specialized meat producing unit" and described as being *adjusted* to meat production, giving an image of an almost natural process (termed "animal improvement") largely without invasive human interference (Henriksson 2000, 165, my translation). Another natural science textbook, Andersson et al. (2000), raises the issue of Belgian Blue in a slightly skeptical manner—but not for ethical reasons: "Is this a 'practical' breed for Sweden, since we are not allowed to give the animals growth hormones? Would other breeds suit us better?" (167, my translation). The same material describes the practice of insemination as "[a] technique that we have accepted. Our cows have in this way changed to become very high-producing both when it comes to meat and milk. They belong to the world elite!" (158, my translation).

The business of intensive "livestock" production has been defined as part of a "food regime" (linkage of food production and consumption to capitalist forms of accumulation and regulation). Meat and dairy-producing corporations have organized themselves into powerful political lobby associations that operate with an interest in advancing their industries rather than from an interest in human nutrition and health (Franklin 1999). As Nibert (2002) remarks, in capitalist society food is produced to generate profit, and in modern agricultural systems meat is mass-produced. It follows that "factory farming" and similar abusive practices are not to be seen as occasional anomalies in an otherwise benevolent food producing system but as a *logical outcome* of this system (Adams 1993). Noske (1997) has described how animals have become incorporated into production technology in the process of mass production. By artificial inseminations, genetic manipulation, mutilation, and other measures, the animal is modified and designed to suit the production system and optimize productivity. Animals, or features of them, that cannot be made productive tend to be eliminated by this system. It is a process of *de-animalization* in which animals are being alienated from their own bodies and bodily products (that have been appropriated by the factory management), from their bodily functions when they are streamlined to become specialized in a certain "skill" (such as producing meat or offspring), and from their natural environment (the ecosystem) (Noske 1997).

In a discussion on animal ethics in a social science class during my field study, one student said that we would be able to feed many more people in the world if we stopped eating meat and instead cultivated crops in the areas now used for grazing "livestock." Her statement highlights the links of intensive meat production and consumption to the world economy. When Third World countries are forced to set apart land for the production of raw materials for the Western animal agriculture industry, food imports become necessary to feed their own population, whose dependence on the West increases (Noske 1997). Franklin (1999) outlines how modern "livestock" production developed out of exploitation of militarily acquired and colonially organized land (frequently involving slave labor) for purposes of economic expansion in the sixteenth through nineteenth centuries. Overstocking and overgrazing quickly degraded the pastures, leading the industry to continuously look for opportunities to appropriate new grazing lands (for instance, virgin rainforests). As a symbol of social progress as well as a tool for capital accumulation, meat has had a function of serving the interests of elite classes over the ages (Nibert 2002), and one consequence of this is the environmental problems generated by intensive animal agriculture (Noske 1997), including climate change. The United Nation's Food and Agriculture Organization (FAO) has recognized the "livestock" sector as one of the top two or three most significant contributors to the most serious environmental problems at both local and global levels (Steinfeld et al. 2006).[5] These aspects, however, were absent in the learning materials I investigated. Only in one textbook (Cronlund 2003) was the extensive meat consumption in the industrialized countries briefly recognized as an environmental threat.

Also the dairy industry is part of the animal-based food regime. DuPuis (2002) and Jönsson (2005) have traced the historical origins of the special position dairy products occupy in the United States and in Sweden, respectively. The National Dairy Council was organized in 1915 in the United States in order to promote dairy products, primarily among schoolchildren, by speeches, distribution of publications, and activities such as poster contests, milk plays, and milk songs (DuPuis 2002). In Sweden, the organization The Milk Propaganda (*Mjölkpropagandan*), formed in 1923, operated in a similar manner with schoolchildren as an important target group and arranged special milk lessons in schools. With the aim of increasing milk consumption, the organization cooperated intimately with the dairy companies and also with the Swedish authorities, which was a politically uncontroversial issue since all political parties took a positive stance toward dairy products. Especially the Social Democratic Party saw free school milk as an important part of a progressive social policy (Jönsson 2005).

The dairy industry has managed to maintain its historically privileged position in Swedish society, which is reflected in the space allotted to milk advertisements in schools. Jönsson (2005) notes that the dairy companies seem to be the only commercial actors that can expose their company names and logotypes more or less free of the restrictions that other companies encounter in schools. In all the schools I visited, milk messages were to a greater or lesser extent allotted space in the physical premises of the school. These messages often carried the name or logotype of an agribusiness or other food (dairy) related company.

One company brand in particular—the dairy company Arla—seemed to dominate the school environment, typically the school canteen areas, encouraging increased consumption of (Arla-produced) milk. At one school, color posters (with Arla's logotype) depicting grazing cows under a blue sky decorated the school canteen, as well as a poster depicting large glasses of milk with the text "smarter, more alert, more fun! The energy drink from arla." An Arla-produced poster depicting a cow saying "I am not only a cow, I am organic as well"[6] conveyed an image that the cows actively endorse their own exploitation (my translations).[7] Arla's presence in the schools was recognized in my interviews with students and staff. A teacher told me about contacts and meetings with Arla representatives, and a student at the same school recalled having seen pictures from Arla in his school canteen.

The canteens were not the only school areas where the presence of Arla was encountered. At the student office at one school, a large poster with the title "Hippology," depicting horses, carried the logotypes of Arla and another agriculture-related actor. A message at the bottom of the poster read as follows: "A greeting from Sweden's most beloved cow /.../ Milk gives you real horse power /.../" (my translation). In learning material on environmental issues used at another school, a section entitled "Food" is illustrated with a photo of a breakfast table with two packages of dairy products. Arla's logotype is clearly visible on both packages (Holm 2003, 52). Also, centrally located in the main hall at the same school, colorful and trendy promotion postcards from Arla promoting the company's new products were freely available for all students to take. One of these postcards depicts a woman of color under a shining sun whose lip has stuck to one of Arla's products, a bottle of cold coffee with milk. Historically, milk has been viewed as an important tool to create national identity, modern progress, and a population of physical fitness and health in both the Nordic countries and in the United States (DuPuis 2002; Jönsson 2005). Since a large majority of the people living outside Northwestern Europe and North America are lactose intolerant, milk could also be used as a tool for emphasizing the supremacy of the white race and the perfectibility of the white body (DuPuis 2002). In Arla's postcards, the need to expand the market of dairy products has created a different strategy, in analogy with the change that has taken place in U.S. milk advertisements:

> Yet there is one significant difference between these ads and the 1920s versions. The old milk ads portrayed one form of physical perfection: white beauty and athleticism. The new milk mustache ads instead portray a wide diversity of people in terms of race and social background, including the comedienne Whoopi Goldberg and the Clinton cabinet member Donna Shalala, both of whom have more than a 50 percent chance of being genetically lactose-intolerant. Yet in the eerie similarity of each picture, the voice of authority ("Got milk?") implies that milk drinking is a universal, everyday practice, no matter what your race, culture, or social background might be. The image is a classic example of the politics of perfection. (DuPuis 2002, 218)

Whereas symbols endorsing milk and meat consumption were permitted by the schools to occupy a range of different spaces in the school environment, vegan or vegetarian messages (to the extent that they appeared at all) seemed to be restricted to certain pre-defined areas, typically student bulletin boards.

From the image of milk as essential for good nutrition, it follows that milk must be available at a low price all the time (DuPuis 2002), and the female (cow's) body needs to be appropriated and put to use in this production. As indicated in one of the school canteens, it is the image of the cow that is used as a primary marketing tool by the Swedish dairy companies. In Jönsson's (2005) analysis, the cow functions as a fetish, in the sense that she evokes a certain reality (or image of reality) by simulating it. The cow in the dairy advertisements represents a yearning for the authentic, the pure, and the real, a yearning for an idyllic agrarian context that has never actually existed (Jönsson 2005). The image hides the actual situation for female animals in the agriculture industry, where their exploitation relies on manipulation of their reproductive system. Cows are kept pregnant so that they can be milked constantly and are killed when their productivity, reproductive efficiency, and profitability ends (Adams 2002). In her ethnographic study of Italian cattle breeding practices, Grasseni (2005) concludes that "Milk and cows are the end products and the focus of investment of farmer and breeder who wish to sell their milk for high prices" (46). The value of the cow in a capitalist order lies in her "genetic capital," which is calibrated by quantifying her functional potentialities. This "industrialization of organisms" (35) is the result of a process of commodification in which the bodies of cows (and bulls) are economically calculated, translated into a set of criteria of "excellence," and inscribed into diagrams, listings, and genetic indexes (Grasseni 2005). In the milk advertisements, however, these arrangements are made invisible.

A Swedish documentary TV program, *Uppdrag granskning* (2005), has examined powerful political and economic forces that influence the special position of milk in Swedish society, as well as its relation to health problems such as child obesity and heart disease. According to the program, the EU-subsidized school milk scheme serves the economic function of disposing of the overproduction of dairy products caused by the milk quotas created to give European farmers a guaranteed income. The surplus dairy products that cannot be sold by the farmers are purchased by the EU and disposed of through, for example, the school milk scheme, protected by the milk lobby, in spite of its potentially detrimental health effects on consumers. Together with the dairy companies, the Swedish Board of Agriculture works for encouraging towns and individual schools to apply for EU school milk subsidies. In 2007, Sweden received around seventy million SEK (approximately twelve million U.S. dollars) as EU subsidies for school milk (*Svenska Dagbladet* July 13, 2008).[8] Also in the United States, the government and the dairy council have collaborated to increase milk consumption in schools as a solution to dairy farm income problems (DuPuis 2002).

The capitalist logic of hunting

Wild animals are subjected to commodification processes (symbolically and materially) in, for instance, trophy hunting and hunting as a form of adventure travel. While these hunting forms were heavily criticized in animal protection classes, the approach was different in the hunter education classroom.[9] There, the success of the hunt was measured and valued by certain quantitative indices that were also viewed as important elements of the pleasure to be derived from the anticipated hunting experience. These quantitative indices included the number of points of the animal's antlers (that will later be transformed into a trophy), the number of animals available for legal killing, and the size of their bodies:

The teacher Martin writes on the whiteboard:

"Moose

(Height): 180-210 cm bull

150-170 cm cow"

"Can you imagine such a big moose?" Martin asks. One student asks: "Have you ever popped one like that?" Referring to the animal by the size of his antlers, Martin responds that "a ten-pointer is the biggest I've shot."

When one student asks "Where are fallow deer found, then?" Martin explains that these animals have increased more and more in number. Another student then comments: "Out and pop 'em." Martin, echoing the student's comment, repeats: "Out and pop them, yes." He writes on the whiteboard: Wild boar—125 kg weight—but also says that wild boar weighing up to two hundred fifty kilograms have been encountered: "Awesome, don't you think. Imagine driving over one of those"…One student, Karl, wonders how many moose may be shot: Are you allocated a certain number of animals that you are permitted to shoot within a specific period of time? Martin confirms this. The number [of animals] depends on the size of the area. Karl asks if the number [of animals] is [counted] per hunting team or per person. Martin replies that if you are on your own, "then you can shoot your moose." Martin develops his comment by explaining that an area produces a certain value and that just now the authorities want more moose to be shot.

The quantitative value markers of hunting also carried gendered connotations. Although a few participants in the hunter education course were female, the jargon in the classroom affirmed the gendered dimensions of hunting:

A student tells an anecdote he has heard about a girl who shot for the first time. The teacher Martin seems to be familiar with the story, and joins in. According to the story, the girl [who hunted] had said "I have shot a little bull." Martin reveals that it was a (big) twenty-seven-pointer. "And she [the hunter] was a girl, right," he emphasizes, adding that the boys' [in the shooting team] egos were probably slightly broken at that time. The boys had asked the girl [who shot the moose] to keep quiet about it.

This classroom observation resonates with previous sociological research on hunting from a gender perspective. Bye (2003) points out that women may be welcome to join the hunting party as long as they comply with the conditions set by the men and as long as their interest in hunting does not threaten the male community. Female hunters are expected to follow the masculine discourse in which hunting skills are measured by the number of animals killed, the size of the animal, and the antlers. In Bye's words, male hunters seek to protect the gendered (masculine) hunting space and find strategies that create a distance from feminine influence. Gunnarsdotter (2005) reports about similar experiences during her participant observations of hunting parties in a Swedish rural community.

The exchange value of hunting as articulated in this classroom took the quantitative indices even further by incorporating the animals in a capitalist logic:

Martin asks his students what they think is the term for a certain animal [deer] "in the prime of his life." Martin gives the answer: "He is called *Capital*," he says, writing on the whiteboard:

"Capital—return

12 points" (referring to number of points of antlers as a marker of "capital")

About the opposite of the term "capital," Martin explains: "He goes in return" (referring to reversed development of body/antlers). One student asks: "Do they all become 'capital'?" When Martin replies that they don't, the student continues asking: "It is not something that all of them achieve?" One of his classmates adds to the question: "How many points will it be for the moose then?" Martin explains further, adding that in Norrland (the northern part of Sweden) they have bigger trophies.

When presented to the students, this perspective opens up new modes of thinking about animals and becomes part of the socialization process of becoming a hunter. While individual animals are valorized in terms of their size, they are, paradoxically, also de-individualized so that one individual can be seen as representing all other individuals of the same species as a collective entity. This is underscored by terms such as "planting in" and "locating out" game, which were used in learning materials as well as in classroom interaction, implicitly equating animals with plants or artefacts. The term "biomass," used in the hunter education textbook *The Hunter School* (*Jägarskolan*; Hermansson et al. 1999)[10] incorporates live animal bodies and plants in a collective quantitative/quantified entity at its most logical extreme, thereby denying them subjectivity.

The terminology constructing animals as a collective (economic) entity, and embedding hunting in a structure of financial relations, was further developed in the textbook *The Hunter School*. In the chapter "Hunting and ethics," the following statement was found:

> Good hunting ethics is to tax the ground on its yield. To overtax is unethical. Not to usurp the biggest possible allotment on the license, without working long-term for big and vital game populations, from which the surplus is taxed, is an example of good hunting ethics. (Hermansson et al. 1999, 252, my translation)

The concept of "taxing" was frequently used as a synonym for shooting animals in the textbook *The Hunter School*, which thus represented animals in terms of an economic and symbolic resource and killing in terms of a routine economic transaction for regulating what is conceived as nature's surplus production.[11] This economic notion was presented already in the introductory sections of the textbook, where the value of hunting was calculated in percentages of "recreation value" and "meat value" (Hermansson et al. 1999, 17). In the hunter education classroom animals are constructed as "game" and "game" is construed as a renewable resource, a production unit whose successful management generates both "meat output" and "pleasures and trophies" for human beings. These constructions help to socially and economically valorize the practices and products of hunting in a kind of distanced relation to nature that was otherwise emphatically criticized in the textbook: Hunting was in the introductory chapter described in terms of an original, "natural" form of interaction with nature that many contemporary "city connected industrial people" have lost (Hermansson et al. 1999, 13-16, my translation).

Conclusions

In this chapter I have argued that a capitalist logic underlies many institutionalized forms of human-animal relations, a logic intertwined with commodification processes that build on domination and objectification, often under the guise of harmonious interspecies co-existence. Animal institutions and practices such as the zoo, the food industry, and "wildlife management" thus produce plenty of contradictory meanings that are reproduced in education in the form of a hidden curriculum, implicitly promoting certain assumptions of the human-animal relation while disguising others. Viewed from this perspective, the human-animal relationship is turned into just another form of merchandise for consumption.

One dimension of the commodification process is the exploitation of certain values extracted from the animals. *Symbolic exchange value* may include the number of antler points (i.e., the size of the trophy), the number of animals killed, and the size and weight of the animal's body in the case of hunting/"wildlife management," as well as the representation of certain profile animal species that can be converted to "zouvenirs" and other commercial strategies in the case of zoos. *Economic exchange value* may include material substances derived from the animal body, such as meat and dairy in the case of animal agribusiness, or use values such as entertainment and recreation in the case of hunting and zoos. Embedded in some of these values are the images and promises of mutual interspecies encounter and harmony that are often adopted in the marketing efforts of the products of the animal economy. These promises may be seen as "utopian moments" that will never be satisfactorily fulfilled but must be consumed over and over again, in line with the commodity capitalism logic (Desmond 1999).

Notes

1. Hanson (2002) points to several similarities between zoos and museums. Museum-trained taxidermists influenced the early visual representation of natural settings in U.S. zoo displays; like museum specimens, zoo animals were intended to evoke an aesthetic appreciation of wildlife, and zoo animals used in art as models for painters should, like those in museum displays, be "ideal" specimens (i.e., healthy males; cf. Haraway 2004b).

2. In Desmond's (1995, 1999) analysis, zoo animal babies also provide the "evidence"

of captive animal happiness within a naturalized heterosexual family discourse whose celebration serves conservative political interests.

3. In her analysis of the giant panda in zoos and in wildlife films, Chris (2006) attributes this animal "symbolic overdetermination" (169) since it has been ascribed exceptional inaccessibility, rarity, popular appeal, and economic and political currency. Coupled with its delicate biological reproduction pattern, the species' survival has been positioned as in need of interventions by Western scientists and their superior technology in a manner that Chris parallels with a form of reinterpreted Orientalism (Chris 2006).

4. I read seven student reports. In some of these I also found perspectives that challenged commodification, such as the fictitious zoo being primarily for the animals' sake (not for humans), and being operated without any profit-making interest.

5. For an analysis of how environmental degradation particularly affects disadvantaged human and non-human social categories within a capitalist framework, see McLaren & Houston (2005).

6. From a Marxist perspective, DuPuis (2002) sees organic food production as just another form of "postindustrial" capitalism where the industry tries to meet new consumer desires for the purpose of greater profits.

7. The creation of "speaking" animals in advertisements has been analyzed by Glenn (2004) as a strategy of the animal agriculture industry to sell its products. The creation of animal "subjects" selling themselves not only conveys an idea that they consent to being eaten or otherwise exploited by humans, but also disguises the violence they are subjected to by the industry. An alternative reality is thereby constructed, hiding the actual reality from the consumers' view (cf. the imagery of "research-friendly" mice in laboratory animal advertisements, conveying an impression of these animals as altruistic "helpers" or "saviors" who consent to being used in research [Birke 2003]).

8. According to the Swedish daily newspaper *Svenska Dagbladet* on July 13, 2008, EU member countries are asked by the European Commission to increase the visual impact of the EU school milk scheme by printing posters (with a minimum letter size of one centimeter) that schools receiving the subsidies are to display in their main entrance. The message of the posters should convey that EU-subsidized milk is served at the school.

9. The hunter education course was an elective course offered at the social sciences oriented school in my field study. It is described in more detail in chapter 6.

10. The textbook was produced by the Swedish Association for Hunting and Wildlife Management, an NGO that organizes Swedish hunters and represents their interests. I was informed by the teacher Martin that the book was to be replaced by a revised edition, but during my field study period the old edition was still used.

11. This representation of nature in Swedish hunting discourse goes back to the nineteenth century when animals were seen as a kind of repository existing for the benefit of the human being (Dirke 2005).

Chapter 6

Killing animals: Struggles for legitimacy

Introduction

Although not all human-animal relations necessarily involve violence, the Animal Studies Group (2006) argues that almost all areas of human life are at some point or other involved in the killing of animals. Schools take part in, and benefit from, the systemic killing in a number of ways, but they are also arenas where the legitimacy of killing animals occasionally is interrogated and contested. This chapter explores how negotiations and normalization of routine killing of animals for various human purposes take shape in school.

Controlling life in the zoo

In the zoo, a way of adjusting the number of animal individuals to an economically feasible volume is the killing[1] of "surplus" animals. This knowledge is part of the education of animal caretaker students, but an "insider" knowledge that the animal caretakers are not supposed to pass on to visitors to the zoo. At one animal caretaker school, after a class of detailed guiding instruction during which the teacher had emphasized that the students must make every effort to avoid speaking about animal deaths and euthanization when they guide visitors, it was time for practice at the school's animal facilities. Next to the bird enclosure, the teacher repeated one of the important points:

> "We will kill some of them [a fowl species]. They will be used as food for the ravens, you understand," the teacher says, and continues: "But we will not mention that [during guiding]!" About the geese the teacher says, "We will slaughter some here as well."

To the outsider, the animal facilities should be presented as an idyllic scene where no human-inflicted (or other) animal deaths occur so the visitors have a positive experience of the site—even if this means disguising the truth of what actually happens to the animals kept there. The "real" zoo logic was to be silenced, remaining as internally shared knowledge between the students and staff. The teacher above explained to his class that the killing of animals at the zoo is part of the park's "economy." An informal interview with Jeanette, a former animal caretaker student, further underscored the killing of "surplus" animals in zoos as a routine, but carefully concealed, aspect of the zoo reality:

> The fact that the baby animals born at the zoo that can't be taken care of are slaughtered is not made known to the public. Jeanette refers to a joke that they [the baby animals] are consumed at the zoo employees' parties.

This killing practice carries several layers of meaning. On the one hand, it may turn animal deaths into "just one more pedestrian detail, unchallenged and rendered unremarkable" (Malamud 2003, B9). On the other hand, the practice also seems to develop certain coping mechanisms among the animal caretakers who transform and incorporate it into an internal jargon, a signifier of "inside" expertise, defining a borderline between the professional in-group and an uninitiated general public. In the process, animals are reduced to entities that can be deemed too many, too few, or adjusted to an appropriate number, but their births and deaths are dealt with differently. Births are exploited in order to enhance the zoo's market value, while deaths are kept behind the scenes, away from the eye of the visitor whose illusion of the zoo as an idyllic Ark must at all times be kept intact.

Killing for consumption: the impasse of meat

Different forms of killing are surrounded by different practices, rituals, and symbolic meanings (Animal Studies Group 2006). In her ethnographic study of slaughterhouse practices in France, Vialles (1994) distinguishes a range of strategies employed to make slaughter morally acceptable and to see the animal slaughtered as something edible rather than as a repulsive corpse. She found a highly complex system of relationships and representations operating inside the slaughterhouse, such as a series of dissociations surrounding the moment of the kill and conceptually keeping it at a distance. Vialles concludes that "meat" is neither the animal nor the corpse of the animal. Through a physical and symbolic process of de-animalizing, the animal is transformed into foodstuff, a substance, with all the links that attached it to a once living body severed.

In school, students encounter on a daily basis the end products of the massive killing of animals for consumption purposes. Neither the vocational animal caretaker programs nor the theoretical programs I visited specialized in food production or the animals within that system and there was therefore no apparent reason to promote any particular food-related values over others in the students' formal education. Despite this, food narratives that offered no real alternative to meat were often prevalent in the students' learning contexts. In this manner, a regulation of eating habits takes place in school. This regulation is productive—it can be seen as an effect of power that actively produces reality and rituals of truth (Foucault 1984).

In the animal protection course, the study material entitled *Animal Ethics* (Jordbruksdepartementet 2003), produced by the Swedish Ministry of Agriculture, was frequently used. One section in the material, entitled "The last journey" (*Grisarnas sista resa*), is a report from a pig farm. The report reproduces a range of elements for perpetuating the hegemonic position of meat (such as toning down the elements of domination and coercion inherent in meat production) while effectively dismissing any counterhegemonic (vegetarian) voices. It does so by applying two main strategies: By depicting a happy narrative of a largely problem-free situation for the pigs destined for slaughter and by refuting a number of *imagined* counter-arguments from voices that are not allotted any space for expressing themselves in the material. The first strategy claims that the pigs themselves actually have something to gain from their position as slaughter animals: "Pigs are bred for the sake of human beings. This is the precondition of their life. Otherwise they wouldn't have existed" (Jordbruksdepartementet 2003, 16, my translation). The second strategy indicates that there is a subordinated critical discourse the text has to act on in order to maintain its convincing power: "Equating animal and human value and ascribing animals human feelings is alien to [Annika, the pig farmer]" (19, my translation).

In one animal protection class, the students were given the assignment to compare information on the Web sites of the NGO *Animal Rights Sweden* and the Swedish meat producers' association *Swedish Meats*. The students were asked to describe their impression of these two Web sites and to discuss them in class. During the discussion, the teacher Sofie encouraged critical analysis of both photos and texts on Swedish Meats' Web site and even employs a form of immanent criticism in her teaching approach by pointing to euphemistic

strategies in the rhetoric underpinning the meat production industry. Nevertheless, the classroom discussion ended by normalizing the killing of animals
for human consumption:

> Sofie expresses with irony in her voice her own impression of Swedish
> Meats' Web site: "The best thing that can happen to a pig is to be
> slaughtered by Swedish Meats! That really is pig heaven!" She asks her
> students if they have reacted to the cute farm and the [agricultural] cycle
> on the Web site. She remarks that they [Swedish Meats] write "The *meat's*
> way" and not "the *pig's* way" from the farm. Sofie encourages her students
> to give critical viewpoints on both Web sites [Swedish Meats' and Animal
> Rights Sweden's]. One student remarks that Swedish Meats wants to
> sell products, but that that is not the aim of Animal Rights Sweden.
> Another student says that if you're a meat farmer, what choices do you
> have? Students' comments on Animal Rights Sweden also argue that the
> organization may generalize bad examples of slaughterhouses, and that
> they try to attract new members. /.../ Sofie asks where the students believe
> the truth is to be found. "In between," the students suggest.

The critique laid out in the situation above is incorporated into a grey zone
in which what is perceived as "extreme" positions on both sides is avoided.
By dealing with the two organizations as if they were equals,[2] the power relations structuring the different conditions in which each actor operates are
obscured. In this manner, the teacher's initial critique is transformed into a
reinforcement of meat production. This position was further maintained by the
extensive teaching about alternatives to *conventional* meat production methods, rather than alternatives to animal agriculture as such, and by the way the
slaughter issue was dealt with in the classroom. The teacher explained "blunders" in the slaughter process (such as stunning failures) by "the human fac-
tor," thus describing animal welfare problems as a responsibility of individual
slaughterhouse workers rather than as a problem inherent in the structures that
make the routine slaughtering of animals for human consumption at all possible. When asked what the reasons might be for "blunders" happening, the
students came up with suggestions such as "lack of manpower, saving money,
pure negligence, and insufficiently educated personnel." By questioning certain practices in the animal agriculture industry rather than the industry as
such, student attention is channelled in the direction of keeping the animal
production system intact.

A school has numerous venues in which to regulate eating habits. In
the schools I visited, this became particularly visible outside the classroom
environment on study visits and excursions when teacher-student interactions
developed in a more informal and (seemingly) less authoritarian atmosphere

as social ties were formed around rituals of eating. Avoiding animal-derived products myself, in these situations I had the opportunity to partake in the actual experience of the minority of students and staff who were vegetarians, rather than just observing how their "deviant" eating patterns were dealt with. Misunderstandings and confusion in planning or pre-ordering of vegetarian meals, vegetarians having to wait for their meals, and other food-related re-strictions (limited supply or even lack of vegetarian food) that applied only to the vegetarians or to those who simply preferred to eat vegetarian foods for the moment, never to the meat eaters, were patterns that occurred with some frequency.

For instance, on a three-day long school excursion during which the re-sponsibility for the purchase and preparation of meals was circulated between small teams of students (under school staff supervision), vegetarian students were largely left to cater for their own food purchases, more or less excluded from the meal community of the larger group. The purchase of food supplies for the excursion was planned in advance by the school staff and carried out in an organized manner at certain selected supermarkets or grocery shops on our way to our final destination. Vegetarian foods were not included in the planning. On these occasions, when the bus stopped, the staff asked that the vegetarians go inside the supermarket and buy their own food, whereas the meat was purchased collectively under the guidance of a staff member. After arriving at our hostel, it became clear that the vegetarians had not been suf-ficiently informed about how many meals they had to plan for, resulting in their quickly running out of food and being reduced to eating the vegetables accompanying the "collective" main (meat) dish.

Lunch the following day was planned as a picnic, and once again the vegetarians were asked to buy their own food. The only vegetarian food found in the grocery store that did not require heating or preparation was bananas and soft cheese, eaten together with potato salad from the "collective" meal, which consisted of various sorts of meat. During the picnic I heard some stu-dents discuss vegetarianism. One student said that she could never be a veg-etarian. Her classmate, a student named Elin, replied that she managed to be a vegetarian for two weeks, then it did not work any longer.

The "deviance" of food choices was thus *imposed* on students by giving them different conditions to the normative food behavior of the larger group. They were subjected to various acts of exclusion from the normal food routines and were marked out by a variety of more or less subtle mechanisms, whereas the "non-option" of meat eating was the unmarked, self-evident, "normal" and natural way to behave that never required further explanation.

During a field excursion, Elin challenged the coercive meat eating rituals. She did this by evoking the formal knowledge she had been taught in another school context—the animal protection course:

> Elin and her classmate Maria sit down beside myself, Bengt, and Kerstin (school staff). Kerstin (the staff member assigned responsibility for the overall meal planning during the excursion) appears proud over the food she planned for dinner, which she refers to not in terms of "the food," but "the meat." Elin remarks disapprovingly that it could be broiler chickens and says with an obstinate voice: "If it is broiler chickens, we'll call Gunilla!" (Gunilla, who didn't join the school trip, teaches the animal protection course.) Elin receives no response from Bengt or Kerstin. The discussion is discontinued. On our way back, Kerstin said to me that it would have been nice to have some red wine with the tasty meat. She does not mention Elin's earlier comments.

Elin breaks an unarticulated social norm by requiring space to make visible the silenced third party in the meat discussion—the slaughtered animal and her previous experiences as a living, sentient being. But there is no such space available. Theoretical knowledge learned in the animal protection course about the situation of animals in the agriculture industry turned out to have little relevance or application to the real, lived relation to animals manifested by Elin's school outside the animal protection classroom. At this moment, these two situations constitute two very separate realities.

When veganism or vegetarianism was discussed in the classroom, the focus was typically on presumed deficiencies in the vegan/vegetarian diet, health problems, and other difficulties and potential threats associated with a meat-free lifestyle (such as the fear that animals will become too numerous if they are not eaten). Positive aspects were rarely raised. Meat, on the other hand, was in general presumed to be a problem-free or even necessary nutrition source for humans. Meat hazards were rarely discussed, although BSE was brought up at a few occasions.[3]

In the learning materials I investigated, vegetarianism or veganism was rarely mentioned, at least not in a positive context. A material on environmental issues was introduced with the following text: "What do you think about when you hear the word 'environment'? /.../ Do you think about politicians dressed in suits, about business leaders or about militant vegans and correctly-fitting shoes? Or do you think about yourself?" (Holm 2003, 6, my translation). The student targeted in this material is obviously not expected to be vegan. In a biology textbook by Ljunggren et al. (2003), vegans are allocated place in the food chain as "herbivores," but the explanation concludes with the characterization of humans as omnivores, thus securing a place for meat in the human diet.

Meat-based and plant-based foods are thus depicted as intimately tied to certain identities and positions. The differentiation is not only endorsed by the school, but the positions are also valorized—usually in support of continued meat consumption. One argument used to legitimate meat consumption relates to biological determinism. Biological determinism builds on the idea that societal norms are based on biological facts (such as biological differences between the sexes) that have their origins in nature and that they therefore must follow what is perceived as "natural laws" so that social arrangements (however oppressive) may thereby be accepted as "natural." In an outline on gender theory, Moi (1997) has shown how the argument of biological determinism has justified subordination of women in society. In the case of human-animal relations, human consumption of animals is often explained on the basis of a biological deterministic logic by deducing human meat consumption from (carnivorous) animal behavior. In this kind of argument, humans are meant to eat animals that are, in turn, meant to be eaten (since animals eat each other). Human consumption of animal flesh is thereby perceived as more or less a "law of nature" rather than an act of choice that reflects primarily a structure of normative meat consumption (cf. Gålmark 2005, 67 on "meat normativity"). An information leaflet about an exhibition entitled *Between us predators* (*Oss rovdjur emellan*) visited by a group of animal caretaker students may be mentioned as an example. The ambition of the leaflet was to refute fears of and prejudices toward "the five big predators" in Sweden (i.e., bear, wolf, wolverine, and lynx. The fifth one, as claimed by the leaflet, is the human being). In this vein, the leaflet states that "We [human beings] are also predators" and in a "fact column" the human being is described as an omnivorous animal and a predator. To underscore and enhance the predatory determinism in humans, a recipe for a reindeer meat dish is included in the text (Elander et al. 2003).

Even the animals kept on the school premises could be ontologized as "naturally" consumable within a framework of biological (or cultural) determinism (cf. Adams 1993). During the introduction week for the new first-year students at one of the animal caretaker schools, I joined a student group on their guided walk through the premises of "the barn":

> At one cage, Mia (staff member) tells the students: "In here we have a Gotland rabbit. Some people eat Gotland rabbits, but we *don't* eat them." Other rabbits are introduced in a similar manner: "These are also meat rabbits, they are very big, you get a lot of meat from them." When we reach the henhouse, Mia goes into the house and comes out with a hen

in her arms. It is a traditional rural breed. Mia explains that this breed has been part of Swedish agriculture for several hundred years, and that it is used in meat production: "There is quite a lot of meat on them," she says as she carefully removes a loose feather from the hen's body. She explains how to hold the hen and says that now we will carry out a health check. "Hi there, now I'll mess with you a little," she says softly to the hen as she shows us different parts of the hen's body and tells us how to check whether she feels well. Mia lets us touch the body of the hen. "Quite a lot of meat on her. From what I have heard, they are supposed to taste great. I'm afraid I have not tried them and will probably not do so either," she remarks.

While the surface structure of the lesson above focused on the hen as a living, sentient subject, the recurring remarks by the supervisor operated in a different direction and conceptually transformed the animal into an inert object predestined for human consumption.

In some of the meat narratives I encountered in the schools, biological determinism overlapped or merged with the idea of "the chain of being," a conception with religious overtones of the universe as a rational, intelligible, continuous order in which nothing is arbitrarily constructed and in which there is for every being an ultimate reason (Lovejoy 1957). This conception could be traced in some of my interviews, such as in the excerpt below from an interview with a teacher, in which the teacher describes how he has dealt with a vegetarian student who has expressed ethical concerns about killing animals in school. His description takes the form of a reconstructed dialogue with the student:

> "Are you going to *kill* all these baby mice?" [the teacher imitates a sobbing student] "/.../ What do you think happens in nature? The snake takes a few, the buzzard takes a few, the fox takes a few. What do you think? [*inaudible*] are you stupid /.../?" She [the student] was resigned. She replied like this, "Yes, of course, if you think about it. But isn't it a little bit sad?" "I don't know if I think that it is sad," I said. "We are born on a planet and as long as we can't leave this planet and some creator, /.../ or some system, has seen to it that we should live in this manner, it is actually the way we live. And in principle, you are a vegetarian. Do you really think it is fair to cut off plants by the roots, you might cut off a life." [The student] had *never* thought about that at all. "What makes you think that a lettuce thinks it is fun to get cut off by its roots?" Complete silence. "I suggest that we don't talk about this anymore, let's move on." She graduated with *very* high marks, very high marks.

Using biological determinism and "the chain of being" as tools for asserting his own authority, the teacher assigns his student to an intellectually inferior position by telling her that her conscientious doubts about killing mice (and, by extension, her vegetarianism) are irrational, inconsistent, and against a natural order.

The logics of biological determinism and "the chain of being" emerged not only in the natural science context. For instance, the pig farmers portrayed in the Ministry of Agriculture's material *Animal Ethics* justified their business with the argument "For [Annika, a pig farmer] it is self-evident that animals are part of nature's cycle where they are also used and eaten by human beings" (Jordbruksdepartementet 2003, 19, my translation). In a written assignment in a social science lesson when the students were asked to reflect on questions in the material, with few exceptions most students stated that meat consumption is natural or even *necessary* for human survival.

The narrative of biological determinism did not always pass by unchallenged in the classroom. In a seminar on animal ethics in a social science class at one of the animal caretaker schools, a student defended human slaughter of animals on the grounds that slaughter has been developed from the animals' own way of getting food. Another student, referred to below, challenged the biological determinism in her classmate's argument, but in the end the discussion was brought back to the stabilizing domain of "humane" treatment of animals in the meat-producing industry:

> We have bred the pigs to produce an additional row of cutlets so that there will be more meat on them. There are incredible amounts of meat, we eat meat almost every day, at several meals a day. It is terrible to see. It is so unnecessary to kill so many animals. We human beings are small creatures, we don't need so much meat. To be an animal friend we would have to take all these animal breeds away, let them die, since they can't manage outside if we release them.

> The student's classmate (who had previously argued in defence of killing animals for human consumption) replies that as it is now, the pigs are not allowed to exercise their natural behavior. It would feel much better to eat meat if they [the pigs] had a better life. I don't understand why they can't legislate so that selling meat is not permitted unless the animals can exercise their natural behavior. The farmers get so many subsidies from the EU.

In a lesson on animal ethics in a philosophy class in the social sciences oriented school, the counterhegemonic argument was voiced by the teacher rather than the students. The general theme of the lesson was the utilitarian philosophy of Peter Singer and the concept of speciesism, and on the basis of this theme the teacher (Johan) initiated a critical discussion of meat consumption. However, he encountered resistance among his students. In the example below, a student claims that animals have no feelings and live according to their instincts, and that therefore eating them is justified. Johan questions the argument, but the discussion still ends with a reinforcement of the meat norm:

> "It is the question of suffering that is interesting, regardless of how developed their emotional life is," Johan says. Another student argues against his teacher: "Eating animals could give their life a purpose." "Is there a purpose with a cow's life, to become an entrecote?" Johan asks with some irony in his voice, and turns to the rest of the class. "What do you say about that?" One student comments sceptically, "That's a good purpose." Another student then raises the issue of painless killing. Johan picks up the philosophy textbook and reads out aloud a long section from it: "But provided that an animal ending up on our plate has been treated well and slaughtered in the right way, it has after all been given a possibility to live a fairly comfortable and carefree life…probably a better life than if it had been living in the wild. The animal would probably not have even existed unless it was bred to be slaughtered. So despite the animal ending up on our plate, the fact that it has been given an existence should mean that the total amount of interests attended to is larger, at least as long as the animal has received good care." (Quoted in Persson 2003, 77-78, my translation)

The message of the story recited by Johan above is that humans act benevolently toward (meat-producing) animals. That this relation is necessarily an unequal one based on dominance and coercion is obscured. The relation is, rather, depicted as a form of social contract of mutual benefit and interest, a win-win situation, where the exploitation of the subordinated is justified as being for her own good (cf. Gålmark 2005, on paternalism). Adams (1993) argues that concern about whether (meat-producing) animals can exist without being destined for slaughter reproduces their ontologized status as exploitable.

Hunter education

The animal caretaker programs included hunting issues in courses on wildlife management and animal protection. In these programs, knowledge and skills in wildlife management/hunting were seen as an important part of animal caretaker professions. At the social sciences oriented school, there was a course in the theory and practice of hunting and two philosophy lessons on animal ethics that included some discussions on hunting. In this school, the hunter education course was an elective course students were able to choose from amongst a range of other "complimentary studies" alternatives and was perceived by teachers and students alike as a learning opportunity that created possibilities for a recreational pastime and for achieving valuable knowledge about animals and nature. It was the second consecutive year that this course was offered and twenty-six students had registered. When I asked the teacher Martin on whose initiative the course was organized, he believed that it was on the initiative of the school principal who, at that time, was in the process of taking a hunter's license himself. The inclusion of hunting as one among many other complimentary study options, such as furniture painting, diving, and taking a driver's license, emphasized hunting as a hobby and equated it with these other activities. For Pernilla, a third-year student in the hunter education class, the course was seen as a way to get easy school credits in what was otherwise experienced as a school with demanding study requirements:[4]

> The workload did not seem too heavy…Schoolwork is heavy now in the end of the third year. /…/ I looked through the entire list of courses from top to bottom to find the one that seemed to be the easiest. I had earlier chosen courses such as furniture painting, and thought that was fun.

In the hunter course syllabus, there is no mention of any critical analyses, and the aims of the course are formulated as providing a background as to *why* hunting and wildlife management are *needed* (emphasis added). Susanne (a non-participant in the course), expressed a different notion about this when I asked her about her reasons for considering taking the course:

> It could be very good to [spend] time out in nature and…get more knowledge about…the countryside…And some want to have hunt-…, protective hunting and so on and then…if you have more facts [you can tell the hunters] you can't shoot here and go moose hunting on this island, instead of not having any knowledge at all. They [the hunters] listen more to somebody who has more knowledge and…knows more.

Seeing the hunter education course as a tool of empowerment to confront hunters and protect animals was, however, an exception among the students I met. Acquiring knowledge about hunting in order to resist it was encouraged neither by the course syllabi nor the learning materials used. In fact in the main course textbook, *The Hunter School* (*Jägarskolan*), hunting was described in deterministic terms by it being an "innate instinct, an original drive" that is "deeply rooted in human nature" (as) our "oldest expression of culture" (Hermansson et al. 1999, 13-14, my translation) and as a "natural" form of interaction with nature. The course textbook expressed this as important for the following "corrective" reasons:

> To many city connected industrial people, the killing shots of the hunter may seem repulsive. They regard the animals as almost immortal and

their conception of reality is not improved by romanticized and distorted nature descriptions in the spirit of Walt Disney. (Hermansson et al. 1999, 16, my translation)

Another learning material justified hunting in terms of fauna preservation, regulation of animal populations, and "enhancing the availability of huntable game" (*Viltvårdskompendium* 2000, 24, my translation). On its cover page, a paradox embedded in the claimed justifications for hunting was acknowledged in a quote from Uncle Jimbo (a character from the animated film *South Park*):

"WE HAVE TO KILL THE ANIMALS SO THAT THEY WON'T DIE!"

Benevolent intervention: Swedish wildlife management

In Sweden, hunting has a long history as a cultural tradition and there are almost three hundred thousand active hunters in the country (Åkerberg 2005). Danell and Bergström (2005) describe the increasing emergence of the ecological perspective in Swedish wildlife management since the late 1960s as a form of all-embracing ideology, nurturing a view of the hunter's mission as intervention in nature in order to adjust "nature's balance." Perhaps for these reasons, Swedish "wildlife management" was normalized in the classroom and largely escaped critique, although other forms of hunting, such as lion hunting in South Africa and British foxhunting, were fiercely criticized (at least in the animal protection classroom). After having shown her class a film entitled *The Hunt*, presenting the heated controversy over foxhunting in Britain, the animal protection teacher Sofie wrote a list on the whiteboard summarizing the arguments of both the foxhunting proponents and the opponents. In this manner she made an effort to give voice to "both sides" of the foxhunting controversy. However, her approach could only be understood as a pseudo action, since other signals, operating in parallel with the surface structure of the lesson, conveyed a different message. When talking about the arguments of the foxhunting proponents, her voice became sarcastic and she pointed out the immanent inconsistencies in their reasoning, thereby rendering their arguments largely invalid:

Sofie tells her class that in many places, the foxes that are hunted (purportedly to keep numbers down and reduce damage) are actually *bred* and that the wildlife management argument is therefore not correct. She further remarks that at the beginning of the film the hunter had a completely different view of the fox than at the end. Sofie continues:

> Some shooting teams go out before the foxhunt and fill up the [fox] burrows. If the fox manages to hide it is no real sport and then the hunters will be disappointed…The discussion ended with teacher and students co-constructing foxhunting as an upper class sport, creating a shared classroom identity in opposition to the foxhunting discourse.

The approach of giving voice to "both sides" was reflected in a written test a week later, where the students were asked to describe the viewpoints of the proponents as well as the opponents of foxhunting, and to outline their own thoughts about the issue. All the students expressed negative thoughts on fox-hunting. Many of them referred to foxhunting as an upper class sport, which was framed as a negative feature, and the fact that foxhunters shoot their hounds when they are not useful in the hunt anymore also provoked indignation among the students, seeing both the hounds and the foxes as being subjected to cruel treatment. Some students imagined themselves in the position of the hunted fox and described how they would feel in this situation. One student even compared the foxhunters to the Nazis in World War II. Another student wrote: "Hunting for pleasure is against human nature, or should be. The only form of hunting that is justified is hunting for food. Killing for pleasure is more like barbarity and all civilized societies should be above this."

Swedish "wildlife management" hunting, on the other hand, was dealt with differently. Johanna, a first-year student, explained to me that prior to the hunting discussions they had in her animal protection class she thought that hunting was always wrong, but now she thinks that animals sometimes have to be shot since we have taken all their predators away and otherwise "billions of roe deer would be running around everywhere." The rationale here is that as long as an animal population comprises a certain number of individuals, hunting is inherently unproblematic:

> "How is it, are there many lynx [in Sweden]?" the teacher Peter asks. He continues: "There are so many that they *can* be shot." He asks how many animals there must be before they can be hunted: At least one hundred animals to get a stable population. When there are two to three hundred animals, hunting can be permitted.

Thus, "wildlife management hunting" was seen as both necessary and accept-able as a way of controlling the ecosystem.[5] The necessity and harmlessness of this form of hunting was further emphasized by positioning it against other more ethically objectionable hunting practices. *Lion hunting in South Africa* was the title of a critical undercover film investigation of "big-game" hunting adventure travel in South Africa that was shown to the students in the ani-mal protection course. Prior to watching the film, the teacher Gunilla used a range of pedagogical approaches to create critical awareness of this particular form of hunting. For instance, she gave her students the task of searching the Internet for information on hunting travel and asked them to find out whether there are Swedish companies selling such trips and at what prices. Gunilla then used the Internet pages her students had printed out in a critical introductory discussion for the film. She talked about the financial interests involved and that the animals are given drugs and kept in enclosed areas to make them easy targets, and also mentioned that students in another class had discussed taking action against the travel organizers. After watching the film, Gunilla asked her class about their thoughts and at the same time expressed her own views: "What does [this film] make you feel like doing? Drugging them [the hunters] and shooting them? I agree."

The critical message concerning this particular form of hunting was clear, but in the film it was also explained that this sort of hunting is far from the annual moose hunt, which has broad popular support in Sweden. Swedish moose hunting is thus justified and framed as primarily unobjectionable and "good" by contrast. An interesting question is what happens when a student challenges this strategy:

> Gunilla asks her class about their reactions to the lion hunting film. /.../ One student, Sara, explains that "I am against hunting, regardless of whether it is about minks or wolverines or what have you." Gunilla then starts to talk about different forms of hunting. "Here, there was cheating on many levels," she says, referring to the film on lion hunting. "What forms of hunting do we have in Sweden?" she asks. "Is it legal to hunt foxes and bears in our country? For some quarry, there are certain [regulated] hunting periods, why is that?" One student replies that there would be too many [animals]. "What happens then?" Gunilla asks. After a student replies, she asks, "What sort of damage do they cause?" One student suggests traffic accidents. Gunilla confirms, *So* many [people] die in crashes with moose, she says, and attempts to summarize the discussion: "OK, then we agree that the [moose] population has to be kept down." Sara, who doesn't accept her teacher's conclusion, objects, "I can't understand why you should kill animals for your own benefit." One of Sara's classmates argues against her: When these animals are hunted, at least the meat can be taken care of. It is not merely trophy hunting. Gunilla gives support to the argument. Another student adds, "There was a list in the newspaper of what animals you are permitted to shoot when at home." Gunilla also adds, "You can take a look at the Web site of the Swedish Association for Hunting and Wildlife Management and get a lot of correct information on regulations."

This classroom interaction indicates that there was a normative framework regulating how to view different forms of hunting. When Sara contested the artificial consensus in the classroom, her perspective was neutralized by a black-and-white picture where the "bad" form of hunting got all the critique and the "good" form was safely protected. Opportunities for re-negotiating this framework were closed off and the voice of authority—the Swedish Association for Hunting and Wildlife Management—was presented as a neutral source of information and was given the final word.

Depending on the context and form of hunting discussed in the classroom, the hunted animals were ascribed different roles. In the case of lion hunting and foxhunting, the animals were constructed as "victims" by teachers and students alike. The film on lion hunting, and the classroom discussions around it, emphasized that the lions are drugged and kept in enclosures to make them easy targets. Further, the film stated that: "Lions are stolen from the [nature] reserve to die without having a chance and end up on the wall of some rich Westerner." Likewise, British foxhunting was framed in the classroom as "cruel," "cowardly," and "barbaric" with wounded animals as a potential risk. When animals are conceptualized as "victims," their sentience as individual beings is placed in focus.

In the case of "wildlife management," the hunted animals were conceived of differently. Moose, for instance, were said to increase too much in numbers and cause different types of harm and problems such as traffic accidents. In a wildlife management class, wild boars were said to enter golf course areas and eat rare orchids, and beavers dig holes in and destroy roads. By positioning certain animals as "problems" or "pests," justifications for killing them are defined. This rationale goes back to the nineteenth century when the Swedish hunting discourse often described hunting in terms of a civilizing project, a fight against "wild nature" and its pests that were considered undeserving of human protection (Dirke 2005).

In order to justify hunting, animals do not have to be conceptualized as "pests." "Game" is another epithet that alone suffices as a signifier of legitimate hunting. In the hunter education classroom, "game" was defined as follows:

"What is 'game,' Jenny?" asks the teacher Martin one of his students. He writes on the whiteboard:

"Game—all wild mammals and birds

Hunting—[to] hunt, catch and/or kill game."

Hunting is often seen as a way of actively inserting oneself into the "food chain" (and thereby achieving a direct connection with nature) (Kheel 1999). Classroom discussions on hunting reflected this idea by focusing on animals as producers of meat for human consumption. In a discussion on animal ethics in a philosophy class, one student remarked that "If we shoot the animals outside and eat their meat, they won't have to experience the [animal] industry," seeing hunting as actually doing animals a favor by saving them from a destiny much worse. For this student, the point is that in the end animals are naturally predetermined to be consumed by humans anyway.[6]

In the hunter education classroom, the learning process involved viewing the animal as a dead object, a lump of meat, even before it is actually hunted (cf. Adams 2002). One element involved in this process was a fragmentation of the animal body, reducing the animal not only to the sum of his/her anatomical parts, but also to an object subjugated to human handling. In classroom interaction, this was expressed as follows:

> The teacher Martin writes on the whiteboard: "Carcass weight"
>
> "What is carcass weight, then, Annica?" he asks one of his students. Annica replies, and Martin comments on her answer: "You have taken out everything [from the animal body], taken away the head and [the flesh] beneath the legs." And you have removed the skin, he adds. (Martin writing on the whiteboard): "Carcass weight: The weight without intestines, lower part of legs, skin, head, about 50%"…Martin says that it is called "carcass weight" since animals in the barn are slaughtered in the same way. "We should be able to shoot 50% of the winter [moose] population," he remarks, adding to what is written on the whiteboard:
>
> "50% shooting
>
> 50%—calf"
>
> One student asks: "How big are the calves, approximately?" Martin talks about the carcass weight of calves. The next question from the class is: "How much can a big bull weigh?" Martin talks about the bull's carcass weight, as well as their weight when alive. "Real beef, right," he says.[7]

In the examples above, animals are dislocated from original states of being, oscillating between their present life in the wild and their future dismemberment as dead raw material, and it is in the interface between these two representations of the animal that a significant part of the hunting discourse operated in the hunter education classroom. In the process, the animal body is almost fetishized as the animal is transformed from living subject into a material and economic object (cf. Kalof & Fitzgerald 2003).

Conclusions

By a range of action-oriented strategies, motivations for the killing of animals for various purposes are productively created and re-created in the school en-vironment. There are certain legitimating conceptions or strategies that seem to facilitate the "naturalizing" of killing animals, to make killing appear mor-ally acceptable and obscure the structural relations of power and domination involved. Examples of such conceptions are "humane" treatment and slaughter of animals and consumption of "organically" produced animal products as well as the logics of biological determinism that conceptually transforms the animal into an inert object predestined for killing (and consumption) even when it is still alive. Another strategy is what Donald (2006) has called the "false alibi," that is, the condemnation of *some* forms of killing in order to vindicate other forms of killing and remove a sense of guilt toward them by positioning them as *not* cruel. The legitimating conceptions and strategies were sometimes de-livered to the students by the school and sometimes co-constructed in teacher-student interaction or among students themselves. Thus, the roles and positions assumed by students and teachers in classroom interaction are complex and do not always imply a straightforward, top-down mediation of values between teacher and students. Socialization into certain human-animal relations of-ten emerges from a context of diverse activities *co-produced* between different actors in school. The analysis of such processes and practices of socialization in formal education helps shed light on the development, consolidation, and reproduction of human-animal relations in society at large.

Notes

1. The appropriate, professional term would be "culling," a euphemism implying that the killing of animals considered dispensable is a practice morally equivalent to the destruction of plants (Bostock 1993).

2. Swedish Meats is owned by farmers with a workforce of 3,800 and annual sales of SEK nine billion (Swedish Meats 2006). Animal Rights Sweden is an NGO with twenty-seven employees (Djurens Rätt 2006).

3. In a discussion on animal ethics in a social science class, a student regarded the "mad cow" disease as positive for the animals in the meat production industry since it resulted in nobody wanting meat from countries other than Sweden anymore due to fear of the disease. BSE was also the subject of an ethology lesson. Although both teacher and students expressed criticism of the animal breeding practices that led to

the outbreak of the disease, the teacher ended the lesson by remarking that when the issue is not raised by media, it is not on the agenda anymore, and you forget about it. She told her class that during a visit to London recently, she ordered veal at a restaurant, without thinking about BSE. In the classroom, meat hazards were thus not seen as a significant reason for choosing a meat-free lifestyle.

4. Even the teacher Martin remarked in a conversation with me that the requirements for passing the hunter education course are not very high.

5. A few teachers, however, critically remarked in the classroom that hunters want to have large populations of animals so that they can get permission to shoot them.

6. The perceived acceptability of hunting animals for their meat led me to expect the issue of indigenous people's "subsistence hunting" to be singled out in the classrooms as the most ethically acceptable hunting practice, but this did not occur in the discussions on hunting that I observed. Rather, these hunting practices were placed in a negative light, for instance, by focusing on whale hunting and bush meat hunting, which were either heavily criticized or otherwise negotiated in the classroom.

7. The word "beef" carries double connotations in Swedish: 1) A muscular body (of a living being); 2) A meat dish prepared for consumption.

PART III

Processes and strategies in human-animal education

In this book I have attempted to critically analyze some social processes and meaning-making practices that form human relations to (other) animals in school. In the animal caretaker programs, where I spent most of my field-work time, animals are at the same time *instruments* and *ends* for learning. They are also components in the development of a professional identity and in the building and strengthening of social ties between (aspiring) members of a professional community. At a more general level, animals are used to create and confirm images of ourselves and the world and are at the same time vehicles for pursuing various worldviews and ideologies (both as embodied beings and as representations).

The social relations I have studied are multifaceted. To summarize, I want to focus on three key aspects: Human-animal *boundary work*, *contradictions* in human-animal relations, and *strategies* used in school to handle potential conflicts emerging around these contradictions. I conclude with a few reflections on the implications of my study.

The animal accessibility rationale: Boundary work around the animal as "other"

This study has shown that schooling not only reflects, but in many respects actively reproduces society's "rationales" for how different animals should be perceived, related to, and used. I argue that these rationales teach the *accessibility* of animal bodies. In this process of social and cultural reproduction, the school must also be engaged in boundary work around the human-animal divide and the image of the animal as *other*.[1] At a concrete level, animal "otherness" is performed in the various ways in which animals are physically put to use in school to achieve certain learning objectives as well as other human purposes (such as nutrition). Even the overarching aim of "saving endangered species" rests on a transformation of animals as individual subjects into generic "others" as species representatives, to conceptualize them as accessible tools for achieving this purpose.[2]

At a conceptual level, boundary work may be part of pedagogical strategies to convey an understanding of animal behavior and prevent incorrect treatment of them and may operate, for instance, in social representations of animals such as the use of *morphisms*, that is, human-animal and animal-machine comparisons. Paradoxically, I have argued that even anthropomorphism, despite its projection of human-like qualities onto animals, ultimately emphasizes human-animal discontinuities through a form of *mimicry* that produces animal subjects that are almost, but not quite, human (cf. Bhabha 1994; Desmond 1999).

Contradiction and conflict

Human-animal relations are imbued with contradictions, expressed not only in the ambivalence of "mimicry" and other forms of identity production. Our ways of observing animals, conceptualizing and handling their bodies, ascribing them social representations and positions and otherwise relating to them, and the institutions we have created for routinizing and rendering efficient these practices, frequently produce contradictory messages. In education contexts, contradiction may be expressed in, for instance, the simultaneous individualization and de-individualization of "game" animals and the financial rationales governing the practice of wildlife management hunting which is nonetheless depicted as an "original" and "natural" activity distanced from industrial society. Other examples of contradiction are the ambivalent responses to captive animals in zoos and the way of presenting "zoo animals" either as representatives of authentic "wilderness" or as volunteering human companions within a commodifying framework that masks coercion and control. Contradiction is also present in the creation of "speaking" animal subjects selling themselves in advertisements of animal industries (cf. Baker 2001; Birke 2003; Glenn 2004). There are numerous other examples, and this study indicates that neither students nor teachers are unaware of these ambivalences, but may articulate and discuss some of them in various situations.

Benton (1993) formulates this condition of ambivalence as an "acute cultural contradiction" of historico-material roots, explained by the co-presence of Western socio-economic practices that reify animals, and representations that assign them quasi-personal status (73). Quoting Thomas (1984, 302-03), Benton even remarks that emerging sensibilities toward the situation and position of animals, together with the material foundations of human society that require their exploitation, present "one of the contradictions upon which modern civilization can be said to rest." Inspired by these analyses, I suggest that the contradictions characterizing human-animal relations in contemporary Western society are driven by a generation of material and symbolic surplus value in which these relations have been increasingly incorporated, and that the contradictions produce different *effects* in different social and cultural contexts, such as the school.

One such effect is that normative presumptions of the "appropriate" position of different categories of animals in society may collide with students' (or teachers') ideas or previous experiences of animals that they bring to the classroom. These (potential) conflicts must be handled by the school in ways that allow for the students' view of themselves as caring and moral actors toward animals to stay intact (cf. Arluke & Hafferty 1996) and at the same time guide students into animal categorization schemes and frameworks that expand the scope of animal accessibility.

Benevolence and inevitability: The production and circulation of "animal stories"

Arluke and Sanders (1996) point out that there are strategies in any culture that provide ways of working around the culture's contradictions so as to overcome possible feelings of discomfort surrounding them and make them appear as a normal part of everyday life. In school, the use of various forms of "motive talk" that morally elevate or neutralize what is done to animals (Arluke & Hafferty 1996) is one example of such strategies. These strategies typically *differentiate* and *valorize* certain social practices of human-animal relations to guide the development of "appropriate" student attitudes toward them.

These strategies furthermore contribute to the articulation of certain *assertions* about human-animal relations, some of which have become fixed and allowed to pass as "truths" (cf. Zeeman et al. 2002). These assertions are recognizable from human-animal discourses in other societal sectors but are reconstituted in school in forms that facilitate smooth accommodation to the animal accessibility rationale. They may be viewed as part of a wider function of the school as a socialization and normalization project and emerge, for instance, in various learning materials, lectures, and other situations of formal and informal interaction. Assertions identified in this book may be grouped under roughly three main themes as follows:[3]

Inevitability (biological/cultural determinism)

• Humans have always eaten meat/hunted

• Hunting is an innate instinct (in the human being)/an expression of culture

• Animals are part of nature's cycle/system where they are also used and eaten by humans

• Humans are predators

• Meat consumption is natural/necessary for human survival

• Animals have no thoughts about the past or the future/live according to their instincts

Benevolence (animals may benefit from their status as "usable")

• One can be a friend of animals, and still eat meat

• If we shoot the (wild) animals and eat their meat, they won't have to experience the (animal) industry

• Animals are no better off in nature (than in captivity)

• Animals are bred for the sake of human beings, otherwise they wouldn't exist

• Eating animals can give their life a purpose

• Provided an animal has been treated well/has had a good life, it is OK to kill (and eat) it

• Zoos help protect endangered species

Common good (practices of animal use may have positive consequences for society)

• If we don't hunt animals, there will be too many of them

• Hunting is OK if the meat is taken care of

• Zoos educate people about animals

Foucault (1993) remarks that "in almost every society there are important stories that are told, repeated and varied; there are ritualized amounts of discourse recited under certain well defined circumstances /…/" (16, my translation). In this book, I have given examples of how the school actively reproduces "animal stories." These "stories," or assertions, about human-animal relations in school constitute a shared frame of reference of commonsense[4] knowledge wherein contradictions usually can be comfortably accommodated (cf. Arluke & Sanders 1996; Baker 2001). If we can speak of a "hidden curriculum" in human-animal education, these "animal stories" are probably part of its foundation, especially if the hidden curriculum is understood as an educational "text" about certain myths and "sacred" beliefs in society (Gordon 1988) that relate to the production of commonsense knowledge (Seddon 1983). Paradoxically, also the animal caretaker education program—which includes goals of professionalization and socialization into a "scientific" way of thinking about animals—frequently seems to rely on the reproduction of commonsensical "animal stories," in effect blurring the demarcation between the two forms of knowledge (cf. Lynch 1988). A possible explanation is that the "animal stories" form a basis of justification for institutionalized animal use, areas of potential future employment for these students. Thus, while the school formally may work to achieve improved conditions for animals in society by professionalization into scientific knowledge about animals, it also performs a contradictory agenda. This agenda consolidates and expands the position of animals as accessible to human use, largely by reliance on commonsense knowledge about animals.

There are also moments when the "animal stories" are challenged and conflicting views of the "appropriate" position of animals in society are raised, negotiated, and contested in school. The conflicts point to a potential fragility in the narratives supporting the position and treatment of animals in society: they need continuous repetition and recreation to maintain authority (cf. Bhabha 1994). Furthermore, the narratives need to present themselves as *benign*, not oppressive (cf. Lundahl, 2005). Consequently, many of the assertions about human-animal relationships identified above were reformulated and repeated in different contexts, sometimes in response to conflicting views, and most of them expressed motivations of either benevolence or inevitability. These processes can be described as a form of species performativity (i.e., consolidation of animal otherness by repeated action over time). They allow students to maintain a sense of self as compassionate actors toward animals, more or less undisturbed by the contradictions embedded in human-animal relations, thus reproducing the image of "benign" oppressive forces at the micro level of the classroom. This understanding helps us see the "animal stories" as they are constituted and circulated in school not as isolated phenomena, but as interconnected parts of a larger social structure.

Concluding remarks

The everyday practices and activities of the schools investigated produce a wide range of meanings about animals and human-animal relationships. These practices may work toward achieving improved conditions for animals in human society, but may at the same time also implicitly consolidate dominant paradigms of utilization and exploitation. I see this as one dimension of the contradictions characterizing human-animal relations in society.

I have argued that practices and rationales of human-animal relations cannot be fully conceptualized in disconnection from the social, political, and historical contexts in which they are embedded. However, with few exceptions, these contexts were rarely explored in the classroom, and if they were, they often became neutralized. When these (and other) educational processes and strategies are analyzed and understood, it also opens a possibility of a reconceptualization of human-animal education. To transform this reconceptualization into educational practice,[5] our education systems need to be equipped to meet challenges such as:

• The notion of the "hidden curriculum": How can it be developed as critical analytical tool for teaching and learning?

• Material and symbolic roots of harmful or oppressive practices: How can they and their effects be critically addressed? And how can alternatives be envisioned and evaluated?

• Intersections and interfaces of various forms of harmful or oppressive practices: How can these be explored while at the same time recognizing the unique circumstances of each form?

Notes

1. This boundary work occasionally reorganizes the human-animal distinction by "othering" certain categories of humans as well, as seen in, for instance, zoos and wildlife films.

2. This does not mean that the individual animal's needs are left unattended to in the process. A core purpose of the animal caretaker education program is to ensure that this does not happen.

3. Similar assertions occurred in empirical data generated by the study that are not presented in the chapters of this book (see, for instance, Pedersen [2008]). Justifications other than those mentioned here include *benevolence*: animals suffer if we don't milk them; medical research (on animals) benefits animals, too and *common good*: medical research (on animals) gives the human being a better and longer life; (medical) testing on animals is cheaper; (animal) breeding can maximize production and help Third World people; the animal industry creates a lot of jobs. An argument that deviated from my categorization is "meat tastes good," justifying meat consumption with the personal pleasure derived from it. See also Hyers's (2006) study of U.S. college students' justifications of different practices of animal use.

4. I refer to a Gramscian understanding of common sense, that is, conceptions of the world that are often fragmentary, incoherent, and inconsequential (Gramsci 2000). Commonsensical conceptions are often contradictory (containing elements of truth as well as elements of misrepresentation) and are accepted and lived uncritically. Many elements in common sense make situations of inequality and oppression appear natural and unchangeable (Forgacs 2000).

5. See Andrzejewski, Pedersen & Wicklund (2009) for suggested curriculum development guidelines for critical interspecies education.

References

Literature, articles, and other sources

Acampora, Ralph. 2005. Zoos and Eyes: Contesting Captivity and Seeking Successor Practices. *Society & Animals* 13(1): 69-88.

Adams, Carol J. 1993. The Feminist Traffic in Animals. *Ecofeminism: Women, Animals, Nature*, ed. G. Gaard, 195-218. Philadelphia: Temple University Press.

———. 2002. *The Sexual Politics of Meat. A Feminist-Vegetarian Critical Theory*. Cambridge: Polity Press.

Adorno, Theodor W. 1974. *Minima Moralia. Reflections from Damaged Life*. London: NLB.

———. 2000. *Problems of Moral Philosophy*. Stanford: Stanford University Press.

Alger, Janet M., and Steven F. Alger. 1997. Beyond Mead: Symbolic Interaction between Humans and Felines. *Society & Animals* 5(1): 65-81.

———. 2003. *Cat Culture: The Social World of a Cat Shelter*. Philadelphia: Temple University Press.

Anderson, Elizabeth. 2004. Feminist Standpoint Theory. *The Stanford Encyclopedia of Philosophy*, ed. E.N. Zalta, Summer 2004 Edition. http://plato.stanford.edu/archives/sum2004/entries/feminism-epistemology/#standpoint.

Anderson, Kay. 1998. Animals, Science, and Spectacle in the City. *Animal Geographies. Place, Politics, and Identity in the Nature-Culture Borderlands*, eds. J. Wolch and J. Emel, 27-50. London and New York: Verso.

Andrzejewski, Julie. 2003. Teaching Animal Rights at the University: Philosophy and Practice. *Journal for Critical Animal Studies* 1(1): http://www.criticalanimalstudies.org/JCAS/Journal_Articles_download/Issue_1/andrzejewski.PDF.

Andrzejewski, Julie, Helena Pedersen, and Freeman Wicklund (2009). Interspecies Education for Humans, Animals, and the Earth. *Social Justice, Peace, and Environmental Education: Transformative Standards*, eds. J. Andrzejewski, M. Baltodano, and L. Symcox, 136-54. New York and London: Routledge.

Animal Studies Group, The. 2006. *Killing Animals*. Urbana and Chicago: University of Illinois Press.

Arluke, Arnold, and Frederic Hafferty. 1996. From Apprehension to Fascination with "Dog Lab." The Use of Absolutions by Medical Students. *Journal of Contemporary Ethnography* 25(2): 201-25.

———, and Clinton R. Sanders. 1996. *Regarding Animals*. Philadelphia: Temple University Press.

Armstrong, Philip. 2002. The Postcolonial Animal. *Society & Animals* 10(4): 413-19.

Baker, Steve. 2001. *Picturing the beast. Animals, identity, and representation*. Urbana and Chicago: University of Illinois Press.

Beardsworth, Alan, and Alan Bryman. 2001. The wild animal in late modernity. The case of the Disneyization of zoos. *Tourist Studies* 1(1): 83-104.

Bekoff, Marc. 2002. *Minding Animals: Awareness, Emotions, and Heart*. New York: Oxford University Press.

Benton, Ted. 1993. *Natural Relations. Ecology, Animal Rights & Social Justice*. London and New York: Verso.

Berger, John. 1980. Why Look at Animals? *About Looking*, by J. Berger, 1-26. London: Writers and Readers Publishing Cooperative.

Bergman, Charles. 2005. Inventing a beast with no body: Radio-telemetry, the marginalization of animals, and the simulation of ecology. *Worldviews: Environment, Culture, Religion* 9(2): 255-70.

Bhabha, Homi. 1994. *The Location of Culture*. London and New York: Routledge.

Birke, Lynda. 1994. *Feminism, Animals and Science: The Naming of the Shrew*. Buckingham and Philadelphia: Open University Press.

———. 1995. Exploring the Boundaries: Feminism, Animals, and Science. *Animals & Women. Feminist Theoretical Explorations*, eds. C.J. Adams and J. Donovan, 32-54. Durham and London: Duke University Press.

———. 2003. Who—or What—is the Laboratory Rat (and Mouse)? *Society & Animals* 11(3): http://www.psyeta.org/sa/sa11.3/birke.shtml.

————, Mette Bryld, and Nina Lykke. 2004. Animal performances. An exploration of intersections between feminist science and studies of human/animal relationships. *Feminist Theory* 5(2): 167-83.

————, and Luciana Parisi. 1999. Animals, Becoming. *Animal Others. On Ethics, Ontology, and Animal Life*, ed. H. P. Steeves, 55-73. Albany: State University of New York Press.

Birkeland, Janis. 1993. Ecofeminism: Linking Theory and Practice. *Ecofeminism: Women, Animals, Nature*, ed. G. Gaard, 13-59. Philadelphia: Temple University Press.

Bostock, Stephen St C. 1993. *Zoos and animal rights. The ethics of keeping animals.* London and New York: Routledge.

Bousé, Derek. 2000. *Wildlife Films.* Philadelphia: University of Pennsylvania Press.

Brock University. 2007. *Call for Papers: Thinking About Animals: Domination, Captivity, Liberation.* http://www.brocku.ca/sociology/conference/.

Burbules, Nicholas C., and Rupert Berk. 1999. Critical Thinking and Critical Pedagogy: Relations, Differences, and Limits. *Critical Theories in Education. Changing Terrains of Knowledge and Politics*, eds. T.S. Popkewitz and L. Fendler, 45-66. New York and London: Routledge.

Burt, Jonathan. 2001. The Illumination of the Animal Kingdom: The Role of Light and Electricity in Animal Representation. *Society & Animals* 9(3): http://www.psyeta.org/sa/sa9.3/burt.shtml.

————. 2006. Conflicts around Slaughter in Modernity. *Killing Animals,* by The Animal Studies Group, 120-44. Urbana and Chicago: University of Illinois Press.

Bye, Linda M. 2003. Masculinity and rurality at play in stories about hunting. *Norwegian Journal of Geography* 57(3): 145-53.

Carabine, Jean. 2001. Unmarried Motherhood 1830-1990: A Genealogical Analysis. *Discourse as data. A guide for analysis*, eds. M. Wetherell, S. Taylor, and S.J. Yates, 267-307. London: Sage.

Chaib, Mohamed, and Birgitta Orfali. 1995. Inledning. *Sociala representationer. Om vardagsvetandets sociala fundament* [Social representations. On the social foundations of everyday knowledge; in Swedish], eds. M. Chaib and B. Orfali, 15-24. Göteborg: Bokförlaget Daidalos AB.

Chris, Cynthia. 2006. *Watching Wildlife.* Minneapolis and London: University of Minnesota Press.

Clark, David. 1997. On Being "The Last Kantian in Nazi Germany." Dwelling with Animals after Levinas. *Animal Acts. Configuring the Human in Western History*, eds. J. Ham and M. Senior, 165-98. New York and London: Routledge.

Crist, Eileen. 2000. *Images of Animals: Anthropomorphism and Animal Mind.* Philadelphia: Temple University Press.

Danell, Kjell, and Roger Bergström. 2005. "Framtidens lösen för jägaren är viltvård." Om viltvården under 1900-talet. *Viltvård, älgar och jaktturism. Tvärvetenskapliga perspektiv på jakt och vilt i Sverige 1830-2000* [Wildlife management, moose, and hunting tourism. Interdisciplinary perspectives on hunting and game in Sweden 1830-2000; in Swedish], ed. S. Åkerberg, 36-73. Umeå: Hållbarhetsrådet.

Davies, Gail. 2000. Virtual animals in electronic zoos: the changing geographies of animal capture and display. *Animal Spaces, Beastly Places: New geographies of human-animal relations*, eds. C. Philo and C. Wilbert, 243-67. London and New York: Routledge.

Desmond, Jane C. 1995. Performing "Nature." Shamu at Sea World. *Cruising the Performative: Interventions into the Representation of Ethnicity, Nationality and Sexuality*, eds. S.E. Case, P. Brett, and S.L. Foster, 217-36. Bloomington: Indiana University Press.

———. 1999. *Staging Tourism: Bodies on Display from Waikiki to Sea World.* Chicago and London: The University of Chicago Press.

Dickens, Peter. 2003. The Labor Process: How the Underdog is Kept Under. *Society & Animals* 11(1): http://www.psyeta.org/sa/sa11.1/dickens.shtml.

Dirke, Karin. 2005. Djur eller odjur? Attityder till jakt och vilt ur ett idéhistoriskt perspektiv. *Viltvård, älgar och jaktturism. Tvärvetenskapliga perspektiv på jakt och vilt i Sverige 1830-2000* [Wildlife management, moose, and hunting tourism. Interdisciplinary perspectives on hunting and game in Sweden 1830-2000; in Swedish], ed. S. Åkerberg, 74-84. Umeå: Hållbarhetsrådet.

Djurens Rätt. 2006. *About Animal Rights Sweden.* http://www.djurensratt.se/portal/page/portal/djurens_ratt/in_english.

Donald, Diana. 2006. Pangs Watched in Perpetuity: Sir Edwin Landseer's Pictures of Dying Deer and the Ethos of Victorian Sportsmanship. *Killing Animals*, by The Animal Studies Group, 50-68. Urbana and Chicago: University of Illinois Press.

Donnelly, Peter. 1994. Take My Word For It: Trust in the Context of Birding and Mountaineering. *Qualitative Sociology* 17(3): 215-41.

Dunayer, Joan. 1999. Sexist Words, Speciesist Roots. *Animals & Women. Feminist Theoretical Explorations*, eds. C.J. Adams and J. Donovan, 11-31. Durham and London: Duke University Press.

DuPuis, E. Melanie. 2002. *Nature's Perfect Food: How Milk Became America's Drink.* New York and London: New York University Press.

Elder, Glen, Jennifer Wolch, and Jody Emel. 1998. *Le Pratique Sauvage*: Race, Place, and the Human-Animal Divide. *Animal Geographies: Place, Politics, and Identity in the Nature-Culture Borderlands*, eds. J. Wolch and J. Emel, 72-90. London and New York: Verso.

Elstein, Daniel. 2003. Species as a Social Construction: Is Species Morally Relevant? *Journal for Critical Animal Studies* 1(1): http://www. criticalanimalstudies.org/JCAS/Journal_Articles_download/Issue_1/ Elstein.PDF.

Emel, Jody, Chris Wilbert, and Jennifer Wolch. 2002. Animal Geographies. *Society & Animals* 10(4): 407-12.

———, and Jennifer Wolch. 1998. Witnessing the Animal Moment. *Animal Geographies: Place, Politics, and Identity in the Nature-Culture Borderlands*, eds. J. Wolch and J. Emel, 1-24. London and New York: Verso.

Falkengren, Jutta. 2005. *Djurens skepnader: Närhet och distans i diskurs och livsvärld*. [Animal Representations: Closeness and Distance in Discourse and Lifeworld; in Swedish.] Lund Studies in Human Ecology 4. Lund: Lund University.

Femia, Joseph V. 1987. *Gramsci's Political Thought. Hegemony, Consciousness, and the Revolutionary Process.* Oxford: Clarendon Press.

Fiddes, Nick. 1991. *Meat: A Natural Symbol.* London and New York: Routledge.

Fien, John. 1994. Critical Theory, Critical Pedagogy and Critical Praxis in Environmental Education. *Action and Action Competence as Key Concepts in Critical Pedagogy*, eds. B.B. Jensen and K. Schnack, 19-57. Didaktiske studier. Studies in Educational Theory and Curriculum Vol. 12. Copenhagen: Royal Danish School of Educational Studies.

Forgacs, David. 2000. Glossary of Key Terms. *The Antonio Gramsci Reader. Selected Writings 1916-1935*, ed. D. Forgacs, 420-31. New York: New York University Press.

Foucault, Michel. 1983. The Subject and Power. *Michel Foucault: Beyond Structuralism and Hermeneutics*, eds. H.L. Dreyfus and P. Rabinow, 208-26. Chicago: University of Chicago Press.

———. 1984. The Means of Correct Training. *The Foucault Reader*, ed. P. Rabinow, 188-205. New York: Pantheon.

———. 1993. *Diskursens ordning*. [L' ordre du discours; in Swedish.] Stockholm/Stehag: Brutus Östlings Bokförlag Symposion.

———. 1994. *The Order of Things. An Archaeology of the Human Sciences.* New York: Vintage Books.

———. 1995. *Discipline & Punish. The birth of the prison.* New York: Vintage Books.

Franklin, Adrian. 1999. *Animals and Modern Cultures. A Sociology of Human-Animal Relations in Modernity.* London: Sage Publications.

Ganetz, Hillevi. 2004. Familiar Beasts. Nature, Culture and Gender in Wildlife Films on Television. *Nordicom Review* 25(1-2): 197-213.

Giroux, Henry A. 1997a. Crossing the Boundaries of Educational Discourse: Modernism, Postmodernism, and Feminism. *Education: Culture, Economy, and Society*, eds. A.H. Halsey, H. Lauder, P. Brown, and A.S. Wells, 113-30. Oxford and New York: Oxford University Press.

————. 1997b. *Pedagogy and the Politics of Hope. Theory, Culture, and Schooling. A Critical Reader.* Boulder, Colorado: Westview Press.

Glenn, Cathy B. 2004. Constructing Consumables and Consent: A Critical Analysis of Factory Farm Industry Discourse. *Journal of Communication Inquiry* 28(1): 63-81.

Gordon, David. 1988. Education as Text: The Varieties of Educational Hiddenness. *Curriculum Inquiry* 18(4): 425-49.

Gramsci, Antonio. 2000. Notes for an Introduction and an Approach to the Study of Philosophy in the History of Culture. *The Antonio Gramsci Reader. Selected Writings 1916-1935*, ed. D. Forgacs, 324-47. New York: New York University Press.

Grasseni, Cristina. 2005. Designer Cows: The Practice of Cattle Breeding Between Skill and Standardization. *Society & Animals* 13(1): 33-49.

Gruen, Lori. 1993. Dismantling Oppression: An Analysis of the Connection Between Women and Animals. *Ecofeminism: Women, Animals, Nature*, ed. G. Gaard, 60-90. Philadelphia: Temple University Press.

Gunnarsdotter, Yvonne. 2005. Vad händer i bygden när den lokala älgjakten möter jaktturismen? *Viltvård, älgar och jaktturism. Tvärvetenskapliga perspektiv på jakt och vilt i Sverige 1830-2000* [Wildlife management, moose, and hunting tourism. Interdisciplinary perspectives on hunting and game in Sweden 1830-2000; in Swedish.], ed. S. Åkerberg, 106-38. Umeå: Hållbarhetsrådet.

Gålmark, Lisa. 2005. *Skönheter och odjur. En feministisk kritik av djur - människa-relationen.* [Beauties and beasts. A feminist critique of the animal-human relation; in Swedish.] Göteborg och Stockholm: Makadam förlag.

Hanson, Elizabeth. 2002. *Animal Attractions: Nature on Display in American Zoos.* Princeton and Oxford: Princeton University Press.

Haraway, Donna J. 1991. *Simians, Cyborgs, and Women. The Reinvention of Nature.* London: Free Association Books Ltd.

————. 2004a. Modest_Witness@Second_Millennium. *The Haraway Reader*, by D. Haraway, 223-50. New York and London: Routledge.

———. 2004b. Teddy Bear Patriarchy: Taxidermy in the Garden of Eden, New York City, 1908-1936. *The Haraway Reader*, by D. Haraway, 151-97. New York and London: Routledge.

———. 2004c. The Promises of Monsters: A Regenerative Politics for Inappropriate/d Others. *The Haraway Reader*, by D. Haraway, 63-124. New York and London: Routledge.

———. 2004d. A Manifesto for Cyborgs: Science, Technology, and Socialist Feminism in the 1980s. *The Haraway Reader*, by D. Haraway, 7-45. New York and London: Routledge.

Hayward, Clarissa R. 2000. *De-Facing Power*. Cambridge: Cambridge University Press.

Hebert, Niels. 2008. Hon fångar djurens blickar. [She catches the gaze of the animals; in Swedish.] *Tidningen Kulturen* issue 2: March 2008.

Held, David. 1980. *Introduction to Critical Theory. Horkheimer to Habermas.* Cambridge: Polity Press.

Hooper-Greenhill, Eilean. 2001. *Museums and the Interpretation of Visual Culture*. Florence, KY: Routledge.

Horkheimer, Max. 1947. *Eclipse of Reason*. London: Oxford University Press. Excerpt taken from eds. P.A.B. Clarke and A. Linzey. 1990 *Political Theory and Animal Rights*, 92-95. London and Winchester: Pluto Press.

———, and Theodor W. Adorno. 2002. *Dialectic of Enlightenment*. New York: The Continuum Publishing Company.

Hyers, Lauri L. 2006. Myths used to legitimize the exploitation of animals: An application of Social Dominance Theory. *Anthrozoös* 19(3): 194-210.

ICAS (Institute for Critical Animal Studies). 2008. http://www.criticalanimalstudies.org/ABOUT_more.htm.

Jensen, Bjarne Bruun, and Karsten Schnack. 1994. Action Competence as an Educational Challenge. *Action and Action Competence as Key Concepts in Critical Pedagogy*, eds. B.B. Jensen and K. Schnack, 5-18. Didaktiske studier. Studies in Educational Theory and Curriculum Vol. 12. Copenhagen: Royal Danish School of Educational Studies.

Jernudd, Åsa. 2000. The Expedition Film: "Just Looking" at Wild Men and Beasts?! *Aura: Film Studies Journal* 6(4): 4-11.

Jönsson, Håkan. 2005. *Mjölk—en kulturanalys av mejeridiskens nya ekonomi.* [Milk—A Cultural Analysis of the Dairy Counter's New Economy; in Swedish.] Stockholm/Stehag: Brutus Östlings Bokförlag Symposion.

Kahn, Richard. 2003. Towards Ecopedagogy: Weaving a Broad-based Pedagogy of Liberation for Animals, Nature, and the Oppressed People of the Earth. *Journal for Critical Animal Studies* 1(1): http://www. criticalanimalstudies.org/JCAS/Journal_Articles_download/Issue_1/ kahn.pdf.

———. 2004. Personal conversation on the Human-Animal Studies listserv (administered by Psychologists for the Ethical Treatment of Animals).

Kalof, Linda, and Amy Fitzgerald. 2003. Reading the trophy: exploring the display of dead animals in hunting magazines. *Visual Studies* 18(2): 112-22.

Kanpol, Barry. 1999. *Critical Pedagogy: An introduction.* Westport and London: Bergin & Garvey.

Kappeler, Susanne. 1999. Speciesism, Racism, Nationalism...or the Power of Scientific Subjectivity. *Animals & Women. Feminist Theoretical Explorations,* eds. C.J. Adams and J. Donovan, 320-52. Durham and London: Duke University Press.

Kheel, Marti. 1999. License to Kill: An Ecofeminist Critique of Hunters' Discourse. *Animals & Women. Feminist Theoretical Explorations,* eds. C.J. Adams and J. Donovan, 85-125. Durham and London: Duke University Press.

Kincheloe, Joe L., and Peter L. McLaren. 1998. Rethinking Critical Theory and Qualitative Research. *The Landscape of Qualitative Research. Theories and Issues,* eds. N.K. Denzin & Y.S. Lincoln, 260-99. London: Sage Publications.

Lovejoy, Arthur O. 1957. *The Great Chain of Being. A Study of the History of an Idea.* Cambridge and Massachusetts: Harvard University Press.

Lundahl, Mikela. 2005. *Vad är en neger? Negritude, Essentialism, Strategi.* [What is a Negro? Negritude, Essentialism, Strategy; in Swedish.] Göteborg: Göteborg University, Department of History of Ideas and Theory of Science.

Lynch, Michael E. 1988. Sacrifice and the Transformation of the Animal Body into a Scientific Object: Laboratory Culture and Ritual Practice in the Neurosciences. *Social Studies of Science* 18: 265-89.

Macey, David. 2000. *The Penguin Dictionary of Critical Theory.* London: Penguin Books.

Malamud, Randy. 1998. *Reading Zoos. Representations of Animals and Captivity.* New York: New York University Press.

———. 2003. How People and Animals Coexist. *The Chronicle of Higher Education* January 24: B7-B9.

Marcuse, Herbert. 1991. *One-Dimensional Man. Studies in the Ideology of Advanced Industrial Society.* Boston: Beacon Press.

Martin, Jane R. 2001. What should we do with a hidden curriculum when we find one? *Philosophy of Education. Major Themes in the Analytic Tradition. Vol. IV. Problems of Educational Content and Practices*, eds. P. H. Hirst and P. White, 453-69. Taylor & Frances e-library.

Marvin, Garry. 2005. Guest Editor's Introduction: Seeing, Looking, Watching, Observing Nonhuman Animals. *Society & Animals* 13(1): 1-11.

McKay, Robert. 2005. "Identifying with the Animals": Language, Subjectivity, and the Animal Politics of Margaret Atwood's *Surfacing. Figuring Animals: Essays on Animal Images in Art, Literature, Philosophy and Popular Culture*, eds. M.S. Pollock and C. Rainwater, 207-27. New York: Palgrave Macmillan.

McLaren, Peter. 1998. *Life in Schools. An Introduction to Critical Pedagogy in the Foundations of Education.* New York: Longman.

———, and Donna Houston. 2005. Revolutionary Ecologies: Ecosocialism and Critical Pedagogy. *Capitalists and Conquerors: A Critical Pedagogy against Empire*, by P. McLaren, 166-85. Lanham: Rowman & Littlefield Publishers, Inc.

Milson, James L. 1990. Museums, Zoos and Aquariums Partners in Teaching and Learning. *Education* 110(4) (Summer): 521-25.

Mitman, Gregg. 1999. *Reel Nature: America's Romance with Wildlife on Film.* Cambridge and London: Harvard University Press.

Moi, Toril. 1997. Vad är en kvinna? Kön & genus i feministisk teori. [What is a woman? Sex & gender in feminist theory; in Swedish.] *Res Publica* 35-36: 71-160.

Mullan, Bob, and Garry Marvin. 1999. *Zoo Culture.* Urbana and Chicago: University of Illinois Press.

Myers, Olin E. 1996. Child—Animal Interaction: Nonverbal Dimensions. *Society &Animals* 4(1): http://www.psyeta.org/sa/sa4.1/myers.html.

———. 2003. No Longer the Lonely Species: A Post-Mead Perspective on Animals and Sociology. *International Journal of Sociology and Social Policy* 23(3): 46-68.

National Agency for Education, The. 2006. Curriculum for the non-compulsory school system Lpf 94. http://www.skolverket.se/sb/d/493.

Nibert, David. 2002. *Animal Rights/Human Rights. Entanglements of oppression and liberation.* Lanham: Rowman & Littlefield Publishers, Inc.

———. 2003. Humans and Other Animals: Sociology's Moral and Intellectual Challenge. *International Journal of Sociology and Social Policy* 23(3): 5-25.

Noske, Barbara. 1997. *Beyond Boundaries. Humans and Animals.* Montréal: Black Rose Books.

Novek, Joel. 2005. Pigs and People: Sociological Perspectives on the Discipline of Nonhuman Animals in Intensive Confinement. *Society & Animals* 13(3): 221-44.

Olssen, Mark. 2004. Foucault and Marxism: rewriting the theory of historical materialism. *Policy Futures in Education* 2(3-4): 454-82.

Palmer, Clare. 2001. "Taming the Wild Profusion of Existing Things"? A Study of Foucault, Power, and Human/Animal Relationships. *Environmental Ethics* 23(4) (Winter): 339-58.

Patterson, Charles. 2002. *Eternal Treblinka. Our Treatment of Animals and the Holocaust.* New York: Lantern Books.

Patton, Paul. 2003. Language, Power, and the Training of Horses. *Zoontologies: The Question of the Animal*, ed C. Wolfe, 83-99. Minneapolis and London: University of Minnesota Press.

Pedersen, Helena. 2008. Learning to Measure the Value of Life? Animal Experimentation, Pedagogy, and (Eco)Feminist Critique. *Global Harms: Ecological Crime and Speciesism*, ed. R. Sollund, 131-49. New York: Nova Science Publishers.

Perlo, Katherine. 2002. Marxism and the Underdog. *Society & Animals* 10(3): 303-18.

Phillips, Mary T. 1994. Proper Names and the Social Construction of Biography: The Negative Case of Laboratory Animals. *Qualitative Sociology* 17(2): 119-42.

Philo, Chris, and Chris Wilbert. 2000. Animal spaces, beastly places: An introduction. *Animal Spaces, Beastly Places: New geographies of human-animal relations*, eds. C. Philo and C. Wilbert, 1-34. London and New York: Routledge.

Pierson, David P. 2005. "Hey, They're Just Like Us!" Representations of the Animal World in the Discovery Channel's Nature Programming. *The Journal of Popular Culture* 38(4): 698-712.

Raji, Remi. 2005. Afrikaner ställs ut i djurparker. [Africans are exhibited in zoos; in Swedish.] *Dagens Nyheter*, July 17.

Ritvo, Harriet. 1995. Categories. *Social Research* 62(3) (Fall): 419-20.

Rothfels, Nigel. 2002a. Immersed with Animals. *Representing Animals*, ed. N. Rothfels, 199-223. Bloomington and Indianapolis: Indiana University Press.

———. 2002b. *Savages and Beasts. The Birth of the Modern Zoo.* Baltimore and London: The Johns Hopkins University Press.

Schnack, Karsten. 1994. Some Further Comments on the Action Competence Debate. *Action and Action Competence as Key Concepts in Critical Pedagogy*, eds. B.B. Jensen and K. Schnack, 185-90. Didaktiske studier.

Studies in Educational Theory and Curriculum Vol. 12. Copenhagen: Royal Danish School of Educational Studies.

Seddon, Terri. 1983. The Hidden Curriculum: An Overview. *Curriculum Perspectives* 3(1): 1-6.

Selby, David. 1995. *Earthkind. A Teachers' Handbook on Humane Education.* Stoke-on-Trent: Trentham Books Limited.

Shapiro, Kenneth J. 2002. A Rodent for Your Thoughts: The Social Construction of Animal Models. *Animals In Human Histories: The Mirror of Nature and Culture*, ed. M. Henninger-Voss, 439-69. Rochester: University of Rochester Press.

Sheard, Kenneth. 1999. A Twitch in Time Saves Nine: Birdwatching, Sport, and Civilizing Processes. *Sociology of Sport Journal* 16(3): 181-205.

Shor, Ira. 1992. *Empowering Education. Critical Teaching for Social Change.* Chicago and London: The University of Chicago Press.

Shukin, Nicole. 2009. *Animal Capital: Rendering Life in Biopolitical Times.* Minneapolis and London: University of Minnesota Press.

Smith, Allen C, III, and Sherryl Kleinman. 1989. Managing Emotions in Medical School: Students' Contacts with the Living and the Dead. *Social Psychology Quarterly* 52(1): 56-69.

Smith-Harris, Tracey. 2003. Bringing animals into feminist critiques of science. *Canadian Woman Studies* 23(1) (Fall-Winter): 85-89.

Solot, Dorian, and Arnold Arluke. 1997. Learning the Scientist's Role. Animal Dissection in Middle School. *Journal of Contemporary Ethnography* 26(1): 28-54.

Steeves, H. Peter. 1999. *Animal Others: On Ethics, Ontology, and Animal Life*, ed. H.P. Steeves, 1-14. Albany: State University of New York Press.

Steinfeld, Henning, Pierre Gerber, Tom Wassenaar, Vincent Castel, Mauricio Rosales, and Cees de Haan. 2006. *Livestock's long shadow. Environmental issues and options.* Rome: FAO.

Stibbe, Arran. 2001. Language, Power and the Social Construction of Animals. *Society & Animals* 9(2): 145-61.

Svenska Dagbladet. 2006. Massajer i Kolmården upprör. [Masai people in Kolmården upset; in Swedish.] August 2. http://www.svd.se/nyheter/inrikes/artikel_340614.svd.

———. 2008. EU:s skolmjölksstöd ryker i varm mat. [EU school milk subsidies withdrawn from hot foods; in Swedish.] July 13. http://www.svd.se/nyheter/inrikes/artikel_1453619.svd.

Swedish Meats. 2006. *Swedish Meats.* http://www.swedishmeats.com.

Tapper, Richard. 1988. Animality, humanity, morality, society. *What is an animal?* ed. T. Ingold, 47-62. London: Unwin Hyman Ltd.

Thomas, Keith. 1984. *Man and the Natural World. Changing attitudes in England 1500-1800.* London: Penguin Books.

Tiffin, Helen. 2001. Unjust Relations: Post-Colonialism and the Species Boundary. *Compromising Post-colonialism(s). Challenging Narratives & Practices*, eds. G. Ratcliffe and G. Turcotte, 30-41. Sydney: Dangaroo Press.

Twine, Richard T. 2001. Ma(r)king Essence—Ecofeminism and Embodiment. *Ethics & the Environment* 6(2): 31-58.

Uppdrag granskning. 2005. Documentary shown in Swedish television (channel 1), August 30.

Vialles, Noëlie. 1994. *Animal to Edible.* Cambridge: Cambridge University Press.

Warren, Karen J. 2000. *Ecofeminist Philosophy: A Western Perspective on What It Is and Why It Matters.* Lanham: Rowman & Littlefield Publishers, Inc.

Wilkie, Rhoda. 2005. Sentient commodities and productive paradoxes: the ambiguous nature of human-livestock relations in Northeast Scotland. *Journal of Rural Studies* 21: 213-30.

Williams, Anna. 2004. Disciplining Animals: Sentience, Production, and Critique. *International Journal of Sociology and Social Policy* 24(9): 45-57.

Willis, Paul, and Mats Trondman. 2000. Manifesto for *Ethnography. Ethnography* 1(1): 5-16. London: Sage Publications.

Willis, Susan. 1999. Looking at the Zoo. The *South Atlantic Quarterly* 98(4) (Fall): 670-87.

Wolfe, Cary. 2003a. In the Shadow of Wittgenstein's Lion: Language, Ethics, and the Question of the Animal. *Zoontologies: The Question of the Animal*, ed. C. Wolfe, 1-57. Minneapolis and London: University of Minnesota Press.

———. 2003b. Faux Posthumanism. The Discourse of Species and the Neocolonial Project in Michael Crichton's *Congo. Animal Rites: American Culture, the Discourse of Species, and Posthumanist Theory*, ed. C. Wolfe, 169-89. Chicago and London: The University of Chicago Press.

———. 2003c. Introduction. *Animal Rites: American Culture, the Discourse of Species, and Posthumanist Theory*, ed. C. Wolfe, 1-17. Chicago and London: The University of Chicago Press.

———. 2003d. Subject to Sacrifice: Ideology, Psychoanalysis, and the Discourse of Species in Jonathan Demme's *The Silence of the Lambs* (with Jonathan Elmer). *Animal Rites: American Culture, the Discourse of Species, and Posthumanist Theory*, ed. C. Wolfe, 97-121. Chicago and London: The University of Chicago Press.

Zeeman, Laetitia, Marie Poggenpoel, CPH Myburgh, and N. Van Der Linde. 2002. An Introduction to a Postmodern Approach to Educational Research: Discourse Analysis. *Education* 123(1): 96-102.

Åkerberg, Sofia. 2005. Inledning. *Viltvård, älgar och jaktturism. Tvärvetenskapliga perspektiv på jakt och vilt i Sverige 1830-2000* [Wildlife management, moose, and hunting tourism. Interdisciplinary perspectives on hunting and game in Sweden 1830-2000; in Swedish], ed. S. Åkerberg, 11-14. Umeå: Hållbarhetsrådet.

Åsberg, Rodney. 2001. Det finns inga kvalitativa metoder—och inga kvantitativa heller för den delen. Det kvalitativa-kvantitativa argumentets missvisande retorik. [There are no qualitative methods—and no quantitative methods either. The misleading rhetoric of the qualitative-quantitative argument; in Swedish.] *Pedagogisk Forskning i Sverige* 6(4): 270-92.

Teaching and learning materials analyzed

Andersson, Eva Lena, Elna Eksell, David Fogelberg, Bo Furugren, Sven Kollberg, Margaretha Lund, Leif Törnqvist, Bengt Weidow, and Lena Widell. 2000. *Naturlära—växter och djur.* [Natural Science—plants and animals; in Swedish.] Stockholm: Natur och Kultur/LTs förlag.

Andersson, Norbert. 2003. *Teknikboken.* [The Technology Book; in Swedish.] Stockholm: Allde & Skytt AB.

Bevare oss väl! [Save us!; in Swedish.] Study material.

Cronlund, Katri. 2003. *Attityd. Samhällskunskap A.* [Attitude. Social Science A; in Swedish]. Stockholm: Bonnier Utbildning AB.

Elander, Magnus, Staffan Widstrand, and Giovanna Jörgensen. 2003. *Oss rovdjur emellan. En familjeutställning om de 5 stora.* [Between us predators. A family exhibition about the big 5; in Swedish.] Exhibition leaflet. Stockholm: Kulturförvaltningen.

Etologi. [Ethology; in Swedish.] Study material.

Fåglar. [Birds; in Swedish.] 2004. Study material.

Henriksson, Anders. 2000. *Naturkunskap B.* [Natural Science B; in Swedish.] Malmö: Gleerups Utbildning AB.

Hermansson, Nils, Herman Huldt, Jacob Boëthius, and Monica Ekman. (Eds.) 1999. *Jägarskolan. Svenska Jägareförbundets kursbok för jägarutbildningen.* [The Hunter School. The Swedish Association for Hunting and Wildlife Management's course book for the hunter education; in Swedish.] Stockholm: Proprius Förlag.

Holm, Fredrik. 2003. *Miljöboken.* [The Environment Book; in Swedish.] Stockholm: Allde & Skytt AB.

Jordbruksdepartementet. 2003. *Djuretik.* [Animal Ethics; in Swedish.] Stockholm: Jordbruksdepartementet.

Ljunggren, Lars, Bengt Söderberg, and Sven Åhlin. 2003. *Liv i utveckling A. Biologi, Gymnasieskolan.* [Life in evolution A. Biology, Upper secondary school; in Swedish.] Stockholm: Natur och Kultur.

Miniförteckning över Sveriges fåglar. 2004. [Mini list of Sweden's birds; in Swedish.] Sveriges Ornitologiska Förening.

Persson, Ulf. 2003. *Filosofi: frågor och argument.* [Philosophy: questions and arguments; in Swedish.] Stockholm: Bonnier Utbildning AB.

Viltvårdskompendium. 2000. [Wildlife management compendium; in Swedish.] Study material.

Index

Acampora, Ralph, 62

"action competence," 18, 45, 55; in the classroom (the fur issue), 49–51; fostering of, 54–55; teaching of, 47–49

"acute cultural contradiction," 118–19

Adams, Carol J., 108

Adorno, Theodor W., 3–4, 12; on zoo architecture, 62–63

"affective neutrality," 37

alienation, 4

Anderson, Kay, 15n5, 62, 84

Andrzejewski, Julie, 3

animal caretakers, 18, 24–25, 36–37, 43n1, 43n4, 99, 123n2; centrality of taxonomy to, 22; creation of social ties within the animal caretaker community, 39–42; education of, 18–19; hazards of, 41; and the "inspection" of animals, 37

Animal Ethics (Djuretik), 23, 25, 28, 31n1, 107

animal ethics, teaching of, 17, 23, 25, 27, 31n1, 47, 54, 68, 89, 107, 109, 114, 115–16n3

Animal Planet, 29

animal protection classes, 57, 81n6, 93; theoretical knowledge learned in, 104

Animal Rights Sweden, 49, 50, 101, 102, 115–16n3

animal "stories," 1, 2, 17–18; production and circulation of, 119–22

Animal Studies Group, 99

animals: animal biographies, 28–29; "animal" as a derogatory term, 4, 7; "animality" of, 18, 19n2; artificial insemination of, 85; cuddling of, 34, 37;–38; "cuteness" of, 31n2, 34; domestic, 72; exploitation of, 3–4, 6; feminist discourse concerning, 5; "food animals," 23–24; identities of, 18; "social positions" of, 11–12; social representations/constructions, 10–11; "speaking animals," 91, 97n7, 118; subjectivity of, 8, 15n6; "trash" animals, 50;

as material signs for gender, race, or cultural identity, 60

Bousé, Derek, 71, 74, 75; critique of wildlife films, 78; on "Darwinian projections," 77; on "false consciousness," 79

Bryld, Mette, 6

Bryman, Alan, 88

Burt, Jonathan, 14, 71

Butler, Judith, 6

Bye, Linda M., 94

capitalism, 4, 84–85; and food production, 89, 97n6. *See also* hunting, capitalist logic of

Chaib, Mohamed, 10

Chris, Cynthia, 78; on giant pandas' "symbolic overdetermination," 97n3

circuses, 84

classroom settings, and human-animal relations, 1; empirical research concerning, 14–15n1; as a means to understanding our own society, 2; theoretical background of, 1–2

colonialism (European), "civilizing" mission of, 6–7; colonial mimicry, 30; "master identity" of colonizers, 7; "offspring" of, 7

"compulsive heterosexuality," 6

"compulsive humanity," 6

Crist, Eileen, 26, 28

critical theory: aim of critical pedagogy, 3; application of to critical animal studies, 3; application of to education, 3; and the development of critical consciousness, 3

cruelty, 4

cultural determinism, 105

"Darwinian projections," 77

de-animalization, 89

democracy, 25

Desmond, Jane, 18, 30, 58, 59, 60, 67, 72, 96–97n2; on the spiritual dimension of viewing animals, 74

desocialization, 33, 43, 43n2

Dialectic of Enlightenment (Horkheimer and Adorno), 3

Dickens, Peter, 4

Disney's Animal Kingdom, 86, 88

dolphins, 24–25; performances by, 66–68

Donald, Diana, 115

DuPuis, E. Melanie, 90, 97n6

eating habits, regulation of, 102–3

ecotourism, 72, 74

Elstein, Daniel, 11

endangered species, 51, 69, 118

Emel, Jody, 83

emotion management strategies, 35–36, 37–38, 42, 45

environmental education, 45–46, 55–56

essentialism, 9

ethology, 115–16n3; classical, 28, 31n3, 35; classical language of, 26; "scientific" ethological vocabulary, 28

European Union (EU), 92–93, 97n8

farm animals (genetically manipulated), as "bioreactors" and "molecule factories," 27

zoos (*continued*)

"tool," 61–64; "people shows" in, 64, 80n1; as pornographic, 62; "real" zoos, 37; representation of animals and capitalism in, 84–85; similarities to museums, 84, 96n1; zoo stories, 84–85. *See also* school-zoo interfaces